Dark Secrets Behind the Mask

Dark Psychology, Body Language, and the Science of Spotting Lies and Influencing Minds.

MIND ACADEMY

© **Copyright 2025 - All rights reserved.**

The content inside this book may not be duplicated, reproduced, or transmitted without direct written permission from the author or publisher.

Under no circumstances will any blame or legal responsibility be held against the publisher, or author, for any damages, reparation, or monetary loss due to the information contained within this book, either directly or indirectly.

Legal Notice:

This book is copyright protected. It is only for personal use. You cannot amend, distribute, sell, use, quote or paraphrase any part, or the content within this book, without the consent of the author or publisher.

Disclaimer Notice:

Please note the information contained within this document is for educational and entertainment purposes only. All effort has been executed to present accurate, reliable, up to date, complete information. No warranties of any kind are declared or implied. Readers acknowledge that the author is not engaging in the rendering of legal, financial, medical, or professional advice. The content within this book has been derived from various sources. Please consult a licensed professional before attempting any techniques outlined in this book.

By reading this document, the reader agrees that under no circumstances is the author responsible for any losses, direct or indirect, that are incurred as a result of the use of the information contained within this document, including, but not limited to, errors, omissions, or inaccuracies.

Contents

Introduction	1
Chapter 1: The Hidden Forces of Influence	6
Chapter 2: The Anatomy of a Lie	15
Chapter 3: Why We All Hide Behind Masks	26
Chapter 4: The Body Never Lies	35
Chapter 5: The Power of the Eyes	44
Chapter 6: Emotional Manipulation: The Art of Playing with Feelings	54
Chapter 7: The Subtle Art of Persuasion	63
Chapter 8: Does Silence Speak Louder Than Words?	74

Chapter 9: 84
Building Your Psychological Immunity

Chapter 10: 95
The Power of Choice: Building a Stronger Mind

Chapter 11: 104
Decoding Their Moves: Identifying Manipulative Tactics

Chapter 12: 114
Walking Away Is the Most Powerful Form of Control

Conclusion 124

Introduction

You've probably heard the saying, "Don't judge a book by its cover," but come on, we all do it. We judge people constantly by how they look, how they sound, and how they walk. Most of us are pretty sure we're good at it, too. We believe we recognize when a person is lying, when they are concealing something, or when they are trying to get us to do something. Maybe you feel you've got it down—like you're so competent you can spot a phony from a mile away.

But the reality. We all wear masks. Some of us do so intentionally, and others wear their masks out of habit. The reality is, each time we encounter someone, we are encountering a part of them. Not the bare, open, naked person they are within the confines of the doors, but the image that they desire to project to the world, such as carrying around a mask on your face, hiding your true thoughts, feelings, and even intentions.

We all walk around with masks one way or another. Maybe you've got a hard shell with a scared heart inside. Perhaps you are being courageous, but actually, you are not. Maybe you're being one way with specific individuals, but otherwise, when alone. It is the nature of people. We all cover parts of ourselves for our own purposes. We wear masks so that we may blend in, so we may not get hurt, or sometimes so that we may manipulate others. We wish to be able to shape how others perceive us, and we will do nearly anything to perfect that picture.

What if you were able to see past all those masks? What if you were able to recognize the subliminal signals that inform you that a person is concealing something from you or trying to guide your ideas and actions? What if you could discover how to find out what the powers are that lie in hiding behind people's decision-making, interactions, and even manipulation of others?

That's what we're embarking on in this book. I will teach you to feel and understand the psychological energies that reside in everyday interactions. We will learn how the body can transmit information without words, how people send information without noise through their eyes, and how you can employ silence as a powerful control tool. I'll demonstrate to you how to read a lie from a mile off and how to read between what individuals are saying and what they intend to say, even when they tell the exact opposite.

But I will not rest there and demonstrate to you how to only notice the subliminal messages being communicated. Instead, I will explain to you how to be immune to manipulation. We have all at some time in our lives been a victim of someone psychologically manipulating us into doing something we did not want to do. From the person trying to guilt-trip you into joining their side to a manipulator who is trying to manipulate a situation, we have all been there. You will learn how to build your psychological immunity so that you can hold fast no matter what others are doing.

There's only so much authority in being able to access the subtlety of the cues that other individuals are broadcasting out there, whether they're trying to lie to you, manipulate you, or simply impact you in some way. And the beauty of it is, once you acquire these skills, you can actually apply them most anywhere in your life—your relationship, your professional relationships, and your social relationships.

I am not going to give you in this book merely a list of deceptions to use to catch a manipulator or a liar. I'm going to show you how to understand the psychology of doing it so you can start using it in your life as well. Knowing how people think and act is one of the best tools you can have. It's like you're decoding a conspiracy code that makes your eyes perceive the world in a way that most people don't even know exists. I've had clients for years who were in abusive relationships, cheating coworkers, or even abusive family members. They believed they were stuck, that they could not move from wherever they were. They had no idea how to guard themselves against emotional manipulation and how to identify the thin lines in which a person was trying to manipulate them. They were always in the backseat playing catch-up rather than in the driver's seat calling the shots.

The greatest thing is, once you understand how these psychological forces operate, you will see them at work. You'll recognize when you're being manipulated, when someone's attempting to influence your decision, or withholding information from you. But better still, you'll be able to use what you've learned to manage your own behavior and response. No longer will you be a passenger in your own life and become the driver.

I have witnessed this firsthand with so many of my clients. When they learned how to read people's body language and the secret psychology of human behavior, their lives were forever altered. They felt safer making decisions, more potent in their relationships, and wiser about how people were attempting to manipulate them. They no longer let other people control their lives and instead took control of their own lives.

The most important thing I want you to understand is that this is not about making you manipulative or a liar. This is all about learning how to care for yourself and make healthier choices. There are all kinds of people in this world who are attempting to manipulate you in some fashion—either consciously or unconsciously. But with the knowledge you'll gain from this book, you'll be able to navigate those situations with confidence and awareness. You'll stop reacting to others and start acting with intention.

Now, all of this can seem a little overwhelming at first. It is a lot to learn, I tell you. Don't worry, though. You don't have to be a mind reader or even an expert psychologist to start using these techniques. All you have to do is practice and take some courage to try an open mind towards new ideas of the individuals and circumstances in your life.

Each chapter within this book is intended to give you what you need to know so that you can understand what's really happening behind the scenes. We will make complex concepts easier to understand so that you can easily get them and begin applying them to your life immediately. When you have completed this, not only will you have learned how to spot manipulation and dishonesty if and when you encounter it, but you will also have learned how to influence others in positive ways that will gain you what you want, without resorting to manipulation or lying.

You're not going to become someone different. It's that you'll be able to see what those other, unseen forces are that manipulate how you respond to the world so that you can live in more confidence, more mastery, and more peace of mind. It's that you'll be able to learn how to protect yourself against being manipulated, and how to connect with other humans on a deeper, more powerful level.

And while I'm at it, I'll walk you through the anatomy of body language, the art of power, and the insidious little things that tip you off when people are lying. You'll see how silence is as powerful as words, how emotional manipulation is done, and how to use what you're about to learn so that you can stay in front of it.

Alright then. So let's get started. The first is to understand that we all have masks—and if you've been exposed to the psychology of the masks, you'll begin to notice the world differently. Let's start, and I'll show you how to recognize the secrets people keep, and teach you the things you need to know to protect yourself and sculpt the world around you.

Chapter 1:

The Hidden Forces of Influence

Did you ever make a decision that, in hindsight, did not really work? You went out and spent money on something on impulse, or you said yes to doing something you didn't particularly want to do. You're not a weak mind, but there was something in the back of your head operating on you. Those are what I call the hidden forces of influence—the stealth psychological drivers that operate on your decisions without you knowing.

Consider how much we want our decisions to be rational, how much we want them to be the result of careful thought. We want to believe that we're in charge, that we're the decision-makers. But it doesn't work that way. Every day we're hit by psychological forces that impact our thinking, our behavior, and even our desires. They infiltrate our decision-making before we're even aware there is one.

Beginning with the commercials that we watch daily, to peer pressure, these subtle forces are always on the move. They make us choose what we would never have arrived at if we were choosing sensibly or otherwise being bullied. In certain situations, they even force us to perform things against our actual values or necessities.

For example, was there ever a point where you've been buying something just because it's on sale, even if you didn't need it? Maybe you've been following the crowd in some circumstances, not because you felt it was the best thing to do, but because everyone around you is. These are just a couple of examples of how the unconscious dynamics are at work.

Throughout this chapter, we will be delving into the psychology behind those influences. We'll see how our brains are pre-programmed to respond to them, why they work so well, and why they have us making choices that we'll come to regret. The better you understand these unconscious forces, the more you'll be able to recognize how they function in your own life, and take back control of your decisions. So let's start peeling away the veil from these unconscious forces and see how they really operate.

How Hidden Psychological Forces Shape Our Decisions

I remember a weekend some months ago. I received a concert invitation from a friend. I was not in the mood for it; I had other issues on my mind, and I had already made up my mind to stay home and unwind for the evening. But for reasons unknown to me, there was something about the invitation that caught me by surprise and somehow coerced me into accepting, and before I even knew it, I was confirming whether I was coming or not. When I got off the phone, however, I was still not sure. Why on earth had I promised to go when I didn't want to? Was I just trying to be happy with my friend? Was I afraid of being left out?

As I lay back to consider it, something sounded right. I was not in fact doing what I wished to do but instead had been controlled by clandestine psychological forces. These non-material forces, although unseen, are strong enough to steer the manner in which we behave in methods of which we have no conception. We may think that we're being reasonable, but by default, our choice is to a great extent in the hands of prejudice, emotion, and social forces beyond our awareness. It was this that got me to understand that I wasn't in control of it. The forces were.

The first force that affected my decision was **cognitive bias.** Cognitive biases are mental shortcuts that our brain takes in the service of keeping things simple when making decisions, but which can lead us astray. One of the most substantial cognitive biases is the anchoring effect. This is when we make the first piece of information stand out. To me, the initial invitation set the whole context. "It's going to be great, everybody's coming," my friend said. My brain immediately went into the mood that the concert would be fantastic if everyone were going. That did not even make sense, because I was not so much thrilled about the concert itself. The social aspect, due to that initial excitement, governed my decision.

Another thinking bias employed was that of **confirmation bias.** When I was determined to go, I went out looking for reasons to justify my going. I started emphasizing the good reasons for going, hanging out with friends, and getting out of the house, without taking into account that I did not feel rested and required a night free from worry. My mind censored against information that opposed going and only uncovered information in favor of it.

Finally, I ended up falling victim to the **availability bias.** It's when we make a decision based on what comes to mind easily. The moment that I had decided to go to the concert, my mind replaced all the good times that I had had from previous concerts that my friends and I had attended, and thus, going out seemed to be more desirable. My mind goes to easy-to-understand examples, and the enjoyment that I had with friends caused me to feel that this experience would be no different, although I hadn't thought so.

Another powerful influence on my decision was **social proof.** Social proof is the psychological effect whereby human beings tend to emulate the behavior of others by reasoning that if a lot of people are doing something, then they must be doing the right thing. It wasn't really that my friend was inviting me; it was that everyone else would be there. To me, the fact that everyone was going to the party made the party more appealing, although I wasn't particularly interested.

Social proof works all the way through our own lives. When we're choosing where to dine, for example, we'll eat in the most popular restaurant because we assume it must be good since there's a crowd of people. We trend after the crowd's action, trusting that they have something we don't. We will then follow suit and make our decision, without even knowing what this decision would be. To me, the possibility of conforming to some crowd and engaging in crowd behavior placed some mild pressure to conform despite being an anti-conformity protest.

The language used in the invitation was also a significant consideration in my decision. This is an example of the **framing effect**, an example of psychological bias where the manner in which we frame and present things to ourselves affects how we react to them. If my friend had only asked, "Do you want to go to this concert with me?" I could have more objectively weighed whether or not I would go. Instead, the invitation was phrased to play up the group element and the "fun" involved, so that I would believe that it would be a fantastic experience I would be mad to miss.

We encounter framing all the time. Take the case of a product advertised as "90% fat-free" and one that says "10% fat content." They both say the same thing, yet one of them sounds considerably healthier than the other. The framing of the data tricks our mind, making us more inclined to base our decision on the way the data is presented, and not on the facts themselves.

These hidden psychological forces decide our choices in ways we don't even realize. From the cognitive biases that contaminate our own judgment to the social pressures that influence us to conform, these forces make almost every choice we make.

The Invisible Hands that Guide Our Choices and Actions

We think we are choosing what we want to do all on our own. The truth is that most of the choice is made by the powers outside our own awareness. These powers outside, other people, situations, and what other people think, push the way we act without us ever even having the understanding to know it. There are these behind-the-scenes hands, making us gently a little in some ways. The moment you realize these forces exist, you can see how they influence you on a daily basis.

Influence of Family and Friends

Possibly the most influential force of our choices is the people we're around. It's simple to think we're choosing for ourselves, but our friends and family, even acquaintances, profoundly impact us. We're social beings. We must belong, be accepted, and be included. And this need to be included can be a terrific help in making us do what everyone else is doing without even realizing it.

For example, think about how fast we change our own schedules due to friends. You don't want to leave the house, but if all of your friends who you know are out doing the same thing, you're likely to end up going anyway. Despite the fact that we know we'd prefer to stay home, the fear of disappointing other people or of being left out will lead us to make decisions we wouldn't usually make. It's a very subtle but powerful influence. We want to fit in, and that's what we do.

Cultural Expectations and Social Norms

We're all growing up in a culture, and cultures have some unspoken rules. Those rules show us how to think about success, happiness, and what we should be doing with our lives. When we're very little, we already know what's "right" from the culture we're in. There's a great expectation, for example, that we go to school, work, and live somehow. Those expectations direct us to what we choose for ourselves without even realizing it.

Let's talk about career choices. We're taught when we're young that it's "successful" to be a doctor, lawyer, or engineer. So perhaps we don't have the same interest, but we're drawn to these fields because society informs us that they're the direction to head in. Thinking that "success" looks one particular way has us on paths that aren't necessarily what we truly desire on a deeper level.

The Power of Authority Figures

Authority figures such as parents, teachers, or celebrities influence our decisions the most. We will probably do what authority figures do or say because we believe that they know better than we do. What an authority figure does or says can influence us more than we can even imagine. Think of how many times we automatically accept at face value what a doctor or teacher says. That's the same thing that happens when we hear a celebrity promoting an object or way of life. We trust them, even though we don't know them. We feel that they possess more knowledge or experience than we do, and that makes us approach a decision differently.

The Influence of Our Environment

The environment we live in—the workplaces we toil in, the homes we live in, the playgrounds we play in—can hold the ability to influence the way we act. A peaceful and organized environment enhances our concentration and productivity, whereas a messy environment results in frustration and disorientation. The environment affects the way we feel, and the way we feel affects the way we act.

The TV that we watch is another powerful environmental force. The movies, TV shows, commercials, and websites we view on a daily basis can affect what we feel, desire, and even what is "normal" to us. When we repeatedly observe some products, lifestyles, or even fashion as the "ideal," we are usually being told to do the same. We are taught in the world around us what is essential, what is "cool," and what we need to work towards without realizing it.

The Role of Social Media

Social media is now one of the strongest outside influences. Every day, just by being alive, we are bombarded with the lives of other people through status updates, images, and videos. This has the potential to widen a gap between the way we perceive ourselves and the way we believe that we count. Exposing ourselves to images of some look, experience, or way of life can pressure us into doing what would not be our personality.

Social media leads us to believe that we need to be similar to other people, even if we don't have an unconscious urge to. Let's say, for example, that all the people you follow on Instagram are talking about some new gym routine or that new restaurant, you would be inclined to go out and try it even if it is not your favorite. It is the desire to belong to the online discussion, to be in the know, that motivates a great deal of our behavior today.

The forces that guide our decisions are most likely not in our conscious mind. Social forces, societal pressures, authoritative figures, our environment, and social media are all guiding us, even if we think that we are deciding things on our own.

Key Takeaways:

- **Psychological forces determine our decisions**: Most of what we decide is driven by invisible prejudice, social convention, and cultural heritage. The reason we know they're there is so we can identify when they're pushing us toward a particular destination.

- **Social pressure affects what we do:** We're likely to be following the crowd or conforming and not even know it. The desire to belong may cause us to act in ways we would not normally act, from what we eat to where we go.

- **Influence through authority impacts us significantly:** We are likely to believe in authority, such as experts or celebrities, and their beliefs may shape our choices. We are likely to emulate them or follow suit, even unconsciously.

As we've discovered, our "own" decisions have a whole lot more behind them. Undetectable forces, softer but strong, push and shove us, determining our choices in ways we're barely even conscious. We're as if we're caught up in some sort of never-ending dance of influence, where we think we're making the decisions, but the rest of the world gets a say.

Now that we've explored how psychological forces influence our daily actions, it's time to take a closer look at something even more fascinating: deception. Lies and half-truths are some of the most powerful tools in the human toolkit. Whether we're aware of it or not, we're all exposed to them.

And in Chapter 2, we will show you the anatomy of a lie—how it is constructed and how to recognize them, whether intentional or not. You'll understand how we lie and get lied to, and it will change your whole perspective. You'll be surprised at how easy it is to deceive the mind.

Chapter 2:

The Anatomy of a Lie

We are all liars. Yes, you read that right. Whether we'd care to admit it or not, lying is a part of the human condition. We all hope that we're better than lies, but the truth is, we all lie, albeit some more than others, obviously. The problem is that lies are not what they appear. We have come to believe that lying can be black or white, an easy "yes" or "no". The world isn't so easily divided.

What the public doesn't realize is that deception doesn't always manifest itself in the form of in-your-face, boldfaced lies. Indeed, some of the most vengeful deceptions use deception so inherently subtle you won't even be aware you are being lied to. Think about it, how many times have you been spoken to something that was not a flat-out lie, but evil in motive? Perhaps it was an omission, a half-truth, or a cleverly worded sentence to mislead. These are the sorts of lies that insidiously work their way into our lives and lie to us without trying.

It's not quite so simple to have a lie trapped in your head as just a broken sentence, like telling someone you're fine when you're not or telling someone you didn't do something when you actually did. Deception is not quite that simple. Lies are not just what we say—lies are what we omit, what we tell ourselves, and what emotions we manufacture to make the deception sound plausible.

Some of the most significant lies are those that appeal to our feelings. The catch is that our feelings make us immune to lies. We ignore contradictions in what a person is saying when we empathize with them, are angry, or are enthusiastic. Liars exploit our feelings and weave tales that sound right even if they may not be so. It's not always a matter of falsifying the facts; it is one of constructing a version of the world that we prefer to believe.

In this chapter, we'll dissect the anatomy of a lie. We'll examine the mental and emotional template for the fantastic potential of deception, and we'll navigate the different forms of lies, what they look like, why we use them, and how to spot them. Prepare to see lying in a new light.

The Cognitive and Emotional Structures of Deception

When individuals consider lying, they automatically assume how easy it is. You lie or you tell the truth. That is all there is to it. The truth is not as easy. A lie is not what words you speak; it is the way your mind frames a story and the way your emotions verify that story to make it sound as though it is the truth. To effectively tackle deception, we are going to split it into two frameworks: the cognitive structure, the thought side of a lie, and the emotional structure, the feeling side of a lie. These two frameworks are so connected that one will be more apt to be validated by the other.

Cognitive Structure: The Thought Side of a Lie

The thought framework of a lie is the construction process. The instant you decide to lie, the brain has to do lots of things together at once. It has to initially determine what the truth you wish to hide is and what the lacuna is to be filled in. It is like defining an opening in a story. The instant the gap can be perceived, the brain begins to construct a substitute model that will merge with the actual world without anyone doubting.

The absolute lie is the plausible lie, and plausibility comes first. If the lie is too unbelievable, it is under the weight of incredulity. That's why lies are not overdone; lies are minor variations on what has happened. If you've failed a course and someone asks you where you were, the logical part of your head is constructing an alibi that works in relation to what they understand and anticipate. You might tell them you were helping your family or were busy with something else. The mind develops this excuse by quickly reviewing what could have taken place and selecting a plausible scenario.

This is then followed by memory management. You have to keep in mind the false information you are lying with, so your story will be consistent. The single lie will be surrounded by an array of little lies. It is mental overload, and it is for this reason that people end up committing mistakes when they lie. Their mental operations get overused.

Another primary feature of the cognitive model is control of detail. Too little detail and the lie will be suspicious-sounding and vague. Too much and it will sound rehearsed. The mind calibrates to get it just right. That is why natural lies will contain just enough detail to make them sound truthful, but no more so as to bring themselves to no more attention than it has to. It is never randomly built, but it is orchestrated, though unconsciously, by us.

Emotional Structure: The Feeling Side of a Lie

The affective arrangement of lies is just as important, for the lie itself only works if the appropriate feelings are there. Think of how many times you've believed people not due to what they do or don't say, but the way they say it, due to the way they look, and due to the way they make you feel. Emotions come into play.

Your brain releases emotional tension when you lie. You might feel guilty, nervous, or even fearful of being caught. This is because lying violates our moral and social norms from a very young age. The brain adjusts to this discomfort very easily. It defers attention from feelings of guilt to relief once the lie has been uttered, if the lie seems to work. That relief lends justification to the action, so that the lie appears to have been worth lying about.

There is also an emotional angle involved, which enables the liar to peddle the story. The effective lie at times requires the liar to fake appropriate emotions for the words. If you wish to make someone believe you are miserable, you can soften your tone, change the look on your face, and even rescale your body into a slower, more sluggish tempo. These behavioral cues are strong because human beings have an evolutionary bias to feel emotion as a broad estimate of truth. Correct feelings compel dishonesty and make it feel real, even though information is never genuine.

Over time, feelings can even habituate the act of lying itself. The more a person lies, the less conscience they develop. The pain of feeling is forgotten and substituted with relief or pride at "having gotten away with it." This makes it instinctive and habitual to lie, which is the reason why some individuals are master manipulators. They become so good that they can control their feelings, or at least conceal them, in order to press on with the lie.

How Thoughts and Emotion Work Together

The most interesting thing about lying is the intertwining of the structure of feeling and thought. The brain can make up the most rational, foolproof lie, but if the liar's feelings toward them—desperate tone, nervous smile, or furtive glance—give away, the lie will fall apart. Feelings can also accompany a poor argument, though. A person who appears sure and calm can be believed when presented with a poor argument.

One excellent example of such collaboration is when somebody lies so that they will not be in trouble. The thought system produces the fabrication, but the emotional system creates fear, innocence, or even anger to act out the fabrication. The two systems work together to support each other. When the emotional performance is credible, the mind starts believing in the lie that it created, reducing discomfort and enabling future ease in lying.

One of them is cognitive dissonance. That's the discomfort you experience when what you are doing doesn't fit what you believe. If you think that lying is bad but you lie anyway, your mind may experience a bit of a shock. To undo that, your feelings step in and justify the lie, maybe you tell yourself that it doesn't hurt anybody, or it is the best you can do. This union of reason and emotion enables the lie to sit so comfortably in your head, even though it goes against your beliefs.

Deception is not merely a simple business of dishonesty. It is a complex cognitive and emotional operation. The cerebral brain generates the script, plots facts, and offers plausibility, while the emotional brain plots guilt, assigns sincerity, and convinces the deceiver and the deceived. These two systems combined provide the anatomy for deception. With this invisible structure to recall, we see more acutely. The other time you hear a story that is ever so slightly off, just remind yourself that a lie isn't necessarily in the words, it's in the ratio of thinking and emotion that makes it believable.

The Different Types of Lies and How They're Told

Lies come in any shape or form. They may be innocent or even outright dangerous. We are lying every day, sometimes without even realizing it. There are tiny and innocent lies, for instance, telling someone that their new haircut looks great when in fact you don't like it. Others are gigantic and have serious consequences. The thing is that in order to identify them and save yourself from being cheated, you should study the kinds of lies. So, let's enter the world of dishonesty and talk about seven types of lies that most of us use.

- **White Lies:**

White lies are the most commonly practiced form of a lie. They are those harmless little white lies we say to avoid hurting someone's feelings or to keep everything going smoothly. These lies are usually told with good intentions. For example, if the other person asks you if you are fond of their new dress, you will say to them, "It looks great!" even though in fact you think they have put on something horrible. You are lying, but you are doing it so as not to hurt their feelings and to avoid your feelings crushing theirs. White lies are typically on the approved list for every circumstance, though in reality, they are still not being truthful.

They are helpful in daily life to keep people in good favor or to avoid hurting someone's feelings.

White lies are dishonest because they are thought to be harmless, but they become a snowball effect in the long run. By lying in order not to hurt someone's feelings, you will keep on telling more white lies to cover up previous lies. It becomes a habit, and you don't even realize you are lying. They may end up developing more complex lies in the long run.

- **Omission Lies:**

Omission lies are slightly more cunning. You don't lie, you simply leave things out. You can leave things out in a bid not to make something sound so bad or to avoid arguments. For instance, if you are late for a meeting and do not wish to say the truth that you overslept and missed a bus, you can simply say, "Sorry, I'm late," and not provide the real reason. The truth is there, but is just not being provided in full.

Omission lies are not always technically false because harm can be done without anyone necessarily speaking anything technically false. The victim of the lie may never have even known that they were being deprived of information to which they had a right. Omission lies are actually more challenging to detect subtly because they do not include the creation of a falsehood. Harm is done by omission.

- **Exaggerations:**

Exaggeration is a form of lying where you're making something bigger than it really is.

This is where you're taking something small and making it bigger. Suppose you caught a fish that was 6 inches long, but you tell your friends that you caught a fish that was 12 inches long, then you've exaggerated the truth. Exaggeration usually has nothing at all to do with lying about facts in any way, but it makes what is real bigger. People exaggerate every day for some reason or another.

Sometimes it is to tell a tall tale or to attempt to get attention. It is one of those little white lies that you do not believe is going to hurt anybody. People know fishing stories are exaggerated, right? Blowing everything out of proportion constantly does hurt your credibility, though. When you're exaggerating everything constantly, people are going to start questioning everything you say.

- **Fabrication Lies:**

Fabrications are completely false stories. This is where one tells an entirely false account, most of the time for personal gain or to make a false impression. These are absolute lies with no link to the truth. You can lie and inform a person that you've been to a high-class function when you've never been miles from there.

This is a lie uttered with the intention to deceive and is usually uttered with the intention of presenting the liar in a superior or more interesting position.

Fabrication lies are hazardous because they completely distort the truth. They can be hard to spot, especially if the liar is good at constructing a credible fabrication. Fabrication liars add to a grain of truth in an attempt to make the falsehood sound valid. But be warned—fabrication lies are corrosive, and they will severely destroy trust.

- **Denial Lies:**

Denial lies are when someone denies the truth. This type of lie is usually spoken when someone is caught doing something wrong, and they do not desire to own up. For instance, when a child is caught with cookies to snack on and they say, "I didn't do it!" when cookies are all over them.

Denial lies are unique in that they do not involve the fabrication of new stories or covering up the truth. Denial lies are a bare-faced denial of the way things are. People who lie this way can't appear to take responsibility for the truth about themselves or what they've done. This is painful in relationships or in the business world because what they're actually saying is, "I won't accept what's true."

- **Social Lies:**

Social lies are said in order to simplify social life. Social lies are falsehoods that we say because we don't want to humiliate someone, or get in trouble, or disrupt the peace. A perfect example is when you're questioning somebody about how their day has been, and then they tell you, "It was great!" while they had a terrible day, then that is a social lie. Social lies are said in such a way that everything is skipped and evaded so that there would be no awkwardness.

These lies do nobody any harm but may create feelings of alienation. People feel they are not able to be so frank in social interaction, and ultimately, this encourages a breakdown in truthful communication. Social lies enable communication, but in some situations might cause misunderstandings or alienation between people.

- **Manipulative Lies:**

Manipulative lies are the most harmful. These are lies uttered with the purpose of manipulating or affecting a person to perform an action. Manipulators lie for a purpose, for instance, to exert power, money, or fame.

For example, you tell someone that they need to do something for you because "everyone else is doing it" or "otherwise something awful will happen." Those manipulations guilt-trip or bully you. Manipulative lies are evil as they strike at your feelings and sense of security.

They lead you to believe you're doing the "greater good," while in reality, you are being manipulated. The manipulator will attempt to employ your trust, sympathy, or fear for the purpose of turning it around on you and compelling you to obey them. This type of lie is complex to detect because it aims to turn your emotions around and make you question your own judgment.

Lies come in a variety of forms, from harmless little white lies to more harmful deceptions. Most crucial to determining them is understanding why they are said.

Key Takeaways:

- **Thought and feeling constitute lies:** Deception includes complex mental operations for building plausible tales and emotional manipulation to get those lies believed. Both systems work in tandem to deceive and convince others (and ourselves).

- **Lies come in various forms:** From harmless white lies to manipulative fabrications. Understanding the different types of lies helps us recognize when we're being deceived. Every lie has its purpose, whether it's to protect, control, or mislead.

- **Emotions are behind a lie:** A lie is a line of words more, but behind the lie are the feelings that lie when uttered. It is these, e.g., emotions of guilt, fear, and relief, that accompany one whilst creating the lie to be credible and harder to detect.

As we have outlined, not all lies are told in words. Lies are carefully crafted, feelings and thoughts, to be a suitable part of the life we want people to think we have. Lies are generally part of an entire system of thinking—a way of thinking in which masks are donned to determine how other people think of us. So far as deception is concerned, therefore, the truth is not necessarily merely hidden behind a lie. It is typically hidden behind a disguise, a disguise that we wear to protect ourselves or to present ourselves in a certain way.

In the next chapter, we will discuss the everyday psychological requirement of masks and how they affect the way in which we interact with other individuals. Masks can affect everything from what happens between people to relationships between people and even the way that we define ourselves. Let's examine more closely why we all wear them.

Chapter 3:

Why We All Hide Behind Masks

Imagine you are entering a room full of people, and the first thing you do is put on a mask.

Not a physical mask, of course, but a mask that hides your true feelings, thoughts, and insecurities. You've done it a few hundred times already and did not even know you were doing it. It's the brazen face when you're not sure of yourself. It's the friendly face when you're tearful on the inside. We all do this, and we don't necessarily know that we're doing it.

This is the frightening part: we're not just fooling everyone else. We're fooling ourselves as well. It is simple to envision masks as a covering that we wear so that we may hide our likeness or save ourselves from judgment, but they play a much more serious psychological role. We wear masks to protect ourselves in a world that is full of too much and that is not certain. Masks are how we deal with the intricacies of social life, where vulnerability or "being the real you" is usually a risk we take with caution. But here is the interesting part: the more we wear them, the stranger to ourselves we become.

Now, before I sound like some crazy idea, let's keep things in perspective. Each one of us has a different mask for a different occurrence. The shy, quiet student who's the life of the party, the introverted, shy individual who's the take-charge leader—the masks we lead with are context-dependent and based on what the world requires of us. We don these so we fit in, belong, or protect ourselves from the possibility of failure or rejection. It's like we carry lots of selves around with us, each one of us built for a specific context.

That's dangerous because not only do our masks change others' view of us, but also our view of ourselves. The more we get stuck in a specific mask, the more we begin to feel that it is indeed us. And gradually, we tend to forget that we even have a face under all the make-up, so to speak. We end up living in a world of projection rather than reality. Why do we do this, then? What is the drive behind this psychological need to conceal?

Here in this chapter, we're going to learn why masks have so much to do with how we live every day, how they affect the way we interact with other people, and how they affect the way we perceive ourselves. You might be amazed at how much of our everyday activity is driven by these masks, and how often we don't even know it.

The Psychological Need for Masks in Everyday Life

Life is theater, and we are all actors. We have a different role each day that we perform on various stages. Our audience is our family and friends or co-workers, and they require us to act. So, we use masks. They are not really masks, naturally. They're emotional and psychological masks that we employ to perform the roles that we do. They assist us to fit in, protect ourselves, and appease other people.

Secondly, these masks are tools. They assist us in navigating the world, cover up for our vulnerabilities, and protect us from exposure to vulnerability. You wear the mask of competence as you walk into a meeting. With your friends, you wear the mask of playfulness and spontaneity. We put on these emotional masks to reassure others and be attuned to what is currently occurring. It is like how an actor has to wear the correct uniform for their character, and we wear these emotional masks so that we can play the right kind of version of ourselves for the people in front of us.

The issue with these kinds of masks, though, is that we get so natural in them that we think that this is who we are. We remain in them so long past a certain point that we've lost the person beneath. It's as if an actor exists in his character's disguise for so long that he's not aware that he's not the character anymore. The character is his reality now. In the same way, if we stay behind a mask for too long, we begin to forget what it feels like to be us without it.

We wear masks to keep ourselves safe from the world. If we are insecure, we don a mask of confidence to hide it. If we are anxious, we don a mask of being calm to hide the craziness we feel inside. The mask safeguards us against judgment and allows us to experience things that we are not yet ready for. Just like an actor employs their mask in order to become their character fully, we wear masks in order to become the character that we think we have to portray in life. No matter where we are, whether at work, at home, or with our friends, the mask is our protection that enables us to make it through the day without showing the real way we feel.

Masks enable us to be part of the group as well. They allow us to be part of society, just like an actor is part of a role. Think about how you behave when you're with your family versus the way you act when you're with your friends. When you're with your friends, you might be presenting the persona of the party-going social butterfly. When you're with your family, you might be presenting the persona of the responsible, serious adult. In both situations, you're in character. The mask that you wear is uniquely tailored to the environment and to the people with whom you are getting entangled.

The issue really begins when the mask becomes too easy. Eventually, you start living inside the character, and the mask is the only you that feels real. Consider an actor who has been on set for years, portraying the same role. Soon, they start to get confused with their character and themselves. They believe that they are their character. In the same way, when we're wearing the mask for so long, we start thinking that's who we are. We forget how to drop the role and just be us.

The longer you wear the mask, the more it will affect your relationship. If you're always wearing a mask, the people in your life are only seeing half of you. They never really get to know the actual you—the person behind the mask. This, eventually, can be the cause of a feeling of loneliness. The people around you may sense that they know you, but the you that they're able to comprehend is only half the person you are. They can't reach the real you, the person that is underneath the mask. In the exact manner, an audience sees only the character of the performer; similarly, your family and friends are seeing only the mask that you've constructed.

Every day, you feel as though you're lost. You wonder if anyone ever really knows you or even knows you yourself anymore. This is where the reality of mask-wearing is exposed. We get used to believing that we live someone else's life, but with only half of it. The mask is protective and secure, but at the same time, it does not allow us to relate to people deeper than ever before. The longer we've been wearing the mask, the harder it is to take off. The actor who's been playing the same part for so long can't learn another part. We all know it's the same when we've worn the mask long enough, we don't know when we've ever felt like ourselves without it anymore. We start to question if the mask is who we are.

How Masks Shape Perception and Influence Social Interactions

I remember when my friend Jake and I spent time with a group of people. Jake was the life of the party. He was the one bringing smiles to all, living his life in his stories with passion, and energizing the party. Everyone viewed him as extroverted, outgoing, and lively. Jake was always the center of attention, and having him near created a carefree, fun atmosphere. What people did not understand was that Jake was not as confident as he seemed.

He maintained the role of the "social, fun guy" because it was easier than showing people the more reserved individual. Jake was shy in real life, and large groups of people drained him. But he was also afraid that if he did nothing at all, no one would ever pay attention to him, or at least they would never find him interesting. So Jake kept up the act, though it was exhausting and stressful. One evening, we were just lounging around after a Saturday night clubbing. Jake wasn't talking much, which was untypical of him.

I asked him what was wrong, and after an age-long silence, he collapsed, "I don't know who I am anymore. I'm always this guy who's fun and outgoing, but I'm not like that all the time."

It's like I've been playing a role for so long, I don't know how to be myself."

That's when it struck me—Jake had been hiding behind a mask so long, he didn't know how to take it off. He had duped himself into thinking his mask was his actual face. The mask was where he hid his insecurities and governed the impression people got of him. The reality is that the truth prevailed; Jake was not just hiding behind a mask to go to parties; he was hiding behind one to protect himself from being judged.

The most surprising revelation was that the mask Jake had on did not just affect the way Jake treated other people, but also how different people viewed him. To everyone around him, Jake was always this outgoing, self-assured person. He was the one one went to if one wished to be amused or to converse. Jake's "fun guy" image had established this presumption in all minds. They knew him as this person, and recognition came with that. They did not get to know honest Jake, the sometimes nervous, shy, or merely in need of a moment alone from being the center of attention.

What really hit home with me was the way that the mask began to bleed over into Jake's own relationships, which he did have. The more he wore the mask, the more he began to feel like he had to be it. He felt like he was only being the "fun, social guy" anymore. It pitted him against himself and also against the person that people thought he needed to be. It wasn't affecting the way he interacted with other human beings—it was affecting his own self-image.

The longer it went on, the more the mask became a cage, not an instrument.

The longer Jake wore it, the more he thought he'd never be able to take it off. He was afraid that if he let others see who he actually was, they would find him dull or not fun to be around. He was so frightened of this that he was stuck in his mask and could not step back and reveal the softer aspect of himself. The issue with masks is that they not only alter the way others perceive us—they alter the way we perceive ourselves. The longer we wear a mask, the more our very self becomes imprisoned within it. We start to believe that the mask we are wearing is really who we are. The longer we play the role, the less we will know what it's like to be the real, unmasked us. The longer it goes on, the more we are perhaps so deep into the act that we forget to look for what life outside of it is.

With Jake, his social butterfly persona had become second nature, so that one could hardly imagine otherwise. He had been playing the character for so long that it became his default response even when he didn't want it to be so. The mask was no longer protecting him—it was eating away at him. The more he wore it, the farther away from himself he got.

Masks are provided to us by society in order to survive socially.

They enable us to belong, not be exposed, and dictate what people know about us. The more we employ them, though, the more they prevent us from relating in a real way. We get trapped in the old personality, which is not who we are in our innermost being. Jake's experience reminds us all that we do put on masks to some extent. They allow us to cope with the pressures and stresses of the world outside, but also stop us from being who we really are. The key is to know when to drop the mask and allow the world to see what we're really made of. When we do so, we may be surprised at how much more we feel we're plugged into others and into ourselves.

Key Takeaways:

- **Masks protect us from vulnerability**: Masking protects us from hurt and rejection because wearing a mask does not allow us to be our true selves, so it is easier for us to cope and feel safe.

- **Masks affect how we're seen:** Our self-perception that we project to the world can significantly affect how others view us. Over time, the masks we wear become so convenient to live with that they start determining who we are.

- **Masks affect our relationships:** When we wear a mask all the time, we can become isolated from others, and it becomes even more difficult to connect on a deep and authentic level with them. The more masks we wear, the less in touch we are with who we really are.

We've avoided here the enduring psychological thirst that underlies masks and how they manage not just what others see of us, but also what we know of ourselves. We shift from one role to the next as social beings, and our masks allow us to cope with expectations and shield us from seeing too much. These masks, though, keep us from relating to other human beings and from knowing who we really are.

Our social capital is richer than what we are doing or saying. More likely than not, the reality of the situation lies in the tiniest detail, such as the way a person walks or the way they react non-verbally. We can be so intent on listening to the words people say, and the body might say what the face conceals. This brings us to Chapter 4, and we learn the way our body communicates and how sometimes words mislead it. Nonverbal signals can tell us what we want to know by deciphering the truth lying underneath the cover.

Chapter 4:

The Body Never Lies

In a memorable scene from Suits, Harvey Specter faces off against a witness in a high-stakes case. The witness is on the stand, testifying, telling them they don't know what happened. But Harvey isn't so convinced. Rather than hearing the words, he's listening to the witness's body. As he testifies, his eyes dart wildly about the room, refusing to meet anyone's gaze, and he shudders slightly with his hands as he squirms in his seat. These slight details inform Harvey of everything he needs to know. The body is in direct opposition to the witness testimony.

Harvey, in full stride, now begins to spew out a string of tongue-lashing questions. The more the witness reacts, the more they start to show giveaways of nervousness—rubbing their face or pulling at their collar, dead giveaway signs of agitation. Harvey keeps pushing, remembering what he knows: this guy is lying. There doesn't even need to be any debate; Harvey's ability to read these little tells gives him the advantage. He knows the body never lies.

This scene demonstrates something crucial: while words can be manipulated or rehearsed, body language often reveals the truth. Our bodies give us away in ways that words cannot. Whether we're nervous, guilty, or hiding something, our physical responses often betray us. In the case of the witness, even though their words tried to cover up the truth, their body revealed the stress, anxiety, and guilt they were trying to suppress.

Here, in this chapter, we are going to provide you with the goal of how to read those subtle cues. It could be eye avoidance, perspiration, or a change of position—each action speaks of something that happens within. Harvey's people reading in Suits was not just in hearing what was being said, it was in seeing that, where tension was involved, the body never let anyone down.

The Subtle Signals Your Body Gives Away When You Lie

We've all been told the old saying "actions speak louder than words," and when we're lying, this is undoubtedly true. Our body is constantly revealing something about what we're feeling, even when we're trying to conceal that feeling behind our words. The truth is, when we're lying, our bodies simply can't help but reveal us. That's why body language is so important—it's the way that our body deals with stress, discomfort, and disagreement. If you're lying, your brain is occupied trying to suppress the truth, and your body is reacting in ways that are often beyond your control.

First of all, you have to acknowledge that the body's reactions to lying are often automatic. They're from within us, and we might not even notice they're occurring. They might be so minute that they'll be nothing at all, but with the proper information in your hands, you'll be able to start noticing these reactions.

Let's start with eye avoidance. Most people believe that if someone is not looking at you, then they are a liar. This is not entirely true. While evading eye contact can be one indicator of lying, it does not always mean the same thing. Liars can also have problems with eye contact, especially if they are hiding something. This is due to the fact that their brain is working very hard to uphold the lie, and thus results in tension. With tension, eyes will naturally avoid the individual they are looking at. But other liars overdo it and try to make solid eye contact so that they can be more convincing, but the problem is intensity. The eyes get too intense, phony, or focused, and that is an indication that something's not right.

Expressions on the face are also a huge giveaway. We want a person to be able to hold back on emotions when they lie, but feelings are complicated to repress, most especially on the face. When we lie, our faces will show precisely what we actually feel. For example, take microexpressions, small involuntary facial changes that don't last any longer than it takes for a split second to occur. These brief expressions can express such feelings as anger, fear, or guilt before a person has time to conceal them. A false smile, for example, would look different from a genuine smile. The natural smile involves the mouth and also the eyes—the "Duchenne smile." The deceiver will sometimes produce a tense smile that happens in the mouth but not the eyes. There is no glint in the eyes.

The body stance can also betray deceit. Liars are also tense and fearful, and this can affect their body position. You will notice that a lying person leans away from you, as if they are trying to push away from the issue. They are doing it because they are afraid and trying to defend themselves physically. A liar also crosses their arms, which is the physical indication of defense. Their body is somehow unconsciously trying to protect them from questioning. They can also exhibit closed body language, like crossing arms and legs or hugging their arms to themselves. Withdrawal signals emotional disturbance.

One of the simplest ways of deception is one of restlessness. When an individual lies, their body gets restless. The hands begin fidgeting, fingers tap on the surface, or one finds themselves touching hair or clothes. They are the bodily response of the body towards the inner strain of a secret hiding. Hands are quite indicative as they are generally used for covering, hiding, or gesturing to support our tales. For example, when the subject is trying to convince you of something, they may wave their hands back and forth or rub their face repeatedly. Fidgeting, foot tapping, and face touching, either the mouth or the nose, are all indicative of stress and are the most common bodily responses to deception. Mouth covering is most commonly an unconscious attempt at hiding the truth.

Another significant response that occurs when people lie is a physical alteration in the process of breathing. Lying is stressful, and therefore, the breathing changes. Liars will start to breathe more heavily or in quick, shallow breaths, too. This is because the body is in fight-or-flight, and the person's autonomic nervous system is overextending itself. Their body is stressed, and their breathing indicates it. If you notice a person speaking and you see them breathing very shallowly and quickly, this can be a sign that they are trying to maintain control but are stressed out.

Sweating is also a sure sign of lies. It's not so much an effect of heat physically—it's that when we lie, our tension level increases, and it causes us to sweat. Where this happens is on the hands, neck, and forehead. When one is lying, their skin will be wet or rather damp. Sweating is a reflexive response to the internal tension they are experiencing as they go on with the lying.

Finally, the voice can give hints. The voice will either quiver or swell when someone is not telling the truth. This is because there is tension in the body, and the person is fighting to keep their feelings under control. The rhythm of speech can also be impacted, with the person stuttering profusely or using shorter and more tense sentences. They can also talk too quickly, hurrying to complete the falsehood, or use very long pauses, struggling to put their words together.

So how do you know when someone is lying? Observe the cluster of these body signals. The body of the liar always betrays what they're saying. If you're able to tune into these signals, you'll start to see the big picture. Lying isn't something the person is saying—it's something the body can't help but convey. Tuning into these little things allows us to see past the words and understand some of the truth behind them.

Reading People: How to Decode Body Language for Lies and Truths

One of the most dramatic real-life applications of body language revealing truth was witnessed in 2004 during the highly publicized Michael Jackson child molestation trial.

The very emotional trial, watched around the globe, put the then-beloved pop star under intense examination. He faced some grave crimes, and his every step, every word, every movement was under scrutiny by millions. His own under oath testimony in court on the witness stand was one of the most scrutinized moments, not just for what he testified to, but for what he did with his body. This trial was able to demonstrate just how much body language can express of what is actually being felt, even where what they have to speak goes against it.

In testifying under oath, Jackson was serene and unflustered. He replied with absolute certainty, with the demeanor that he was at ease. On the outside, whatever he had to say was clearly stated to present an image of innocence. However, beyond being in control of his verbal communication, his body language told a different story altogether. The session was a bitter reminder of how body language speaks so much when trying to lie or hide the truth.

Some of the first noticeable things were how Jackson's eye would move. As he answered questions, his gaze would flash across the whole courtroom, never once even glancing at jurors or lawyers. Even though his words were strong, not making eye contact said a great deal. Liars do not wish to glance directly into an individual's eyes because it gives the impression of being naked. Eyes are said to be the "windows to the soul," and when someone is lying, they might feel that eye contact will make it more difficult to conceal their inner mind. Jackson's frantic scanning of the room with his eyes was a dead giveaway that he was nervous and trying to steer clear of the sort of attention entailed by making eye contact.

It was no guess; eye aversion has been placed at the very top of the list of conclusive indicators of falsehood by scientific research. Liars believe that deceptions would be found out by a look. Jackson's failure to maintain eye contact was an unconscious sign that his seeming confidence was a bluff to cover up the nervousness that he was suffering. It made his otherwise composed demeanor incompatible with his restlessness.

And then his body language, too, which contradicted the cool image he was trying to project. When answering questions, his shoulders hunched over, and his body turned away from the lawyers. Rather than leaning forward to answer the questions and project confidence, Jackson leaned back naturally. This is the usual defensiveness in body language.

When one is threatened or uncomfortable, they may physically position themselves away from the situation. Jackson's body was unconsciously expressing his unease with the topic when he leaned back. He did not want to confront it head-on, and his body was trying to get away from it. His words were strong, but his body language showed that he was emotionally distancing himself—there was inconsistency between what he was expressing and what his body was showing.

And another revealing one was when Jackson was asked about his interactions with kids. His response, while calming on initial impression, was a handful. He began touching his face repeatedly, one of the strongest body language indicators of discomfort. Face covering or fidgeting when speaking is usually an unconscious attempt to hide the truth, and it's a characteristic that most cheats possess. The body attempts to conceal the truth, and touching one's face provides a physical shield from the destructive emotions that are evoked. The more forcefully Jackson defended himself on the charges, the more he intruded into his face, particularly into the region around his mouth and nose, which are generally synonymous with hiding feelings.

The more forcefully Jackson tried to convey innocence on his behalf verbally, the more his body pushed him back with these reflex actions. Concern or attempting to persuade individuals of something that is not true can be expressed through the use of hand gestures, especially if overused or used randomly. The inconsistency between what Jackson had been talking about and the concerned gestures that he was using demonstrated the internal conflict within him. It then became clear that although his words were trying to narrate the tale of an innocent man, his body was telling a very different one.

Here's a lesson: while words may be invented, body language is much harder to conceal. The body signals—whether they're direction of gaze, posture, or movement—are most often reflexive reactions to internal sensation. Regardless of how diligently an individual tries to suppress emotions, the body will betray the person. In Jackson's situation, his inability to maintain eye contact, defensive stance of the body, and fidgeting hand movement were all indicators that his feelings were anything but what he was trying to convey on the stand.

When we are stressed, anxious, or guilty, the body will react in ways words cannot cover. It is a split-second physical reaction to the emotional weight of the problem. The moment you start observing these signs, you can already begin to analyze what someone really feels or thinks when their words are trying to deceive you. Jackson's trial was the final evidence of how body language can be so powerful in revealing hidden truths.

This illustrates the worth of understanding how body language works in interpreting people. From the pressure cooker of the courtroom to the water cooler, you can become skilled at reading these signs so that you have a better idea of how people are feeling and why. It is a skill that can penetrate when words cannot.

Key Takeaways:

- **Body language will betray our words:** Our body betrays these little cues, like crossing arms, fidgeting, or avoiding eye contact, that tell us how we really feel. Body language cues can generally say more than the actual words.

- **Stress generates body reactions:** When somebody lies or is anxious, the body reacts involuntarily in the form of shallow breathing, facial spasms, or fidgeting. These body reactions will tell you if someone is lying to you.

- **Notice the cluster of cues:** One cue by itself will not tell us very much, but taken along with other hints, body language tells us a lot about what a person is going to do and feel. Several cues are stronger than one.

We examined how the body tends to reveal what words are trying to conceal in this chapter. Body language is a reliable lie detector and mood watcher. Whether it's a nervous gesture or a slight facial expression, the body can't help but give us away.

Now that we've learned to decode the subtle signals people give off, we're ready to take a closer look at one of the most telling aspects of non-verbal communication—the eyes. Our eyes don't just convey emotion; they can reveal the truth or hide it. In the next chapter, we'll get into the power of eye movements and how manipulators use eye contact to control conversations. Understanding the messages our eyes send can provide insight into someone's true thoughts and feelings, making it easier to spot a lie.

Chapter 5:

The Power of the Eyes

When you think about communication, you might first consider the words we speak. However, the most telling signals often come from our eyes. Eyes have an incredible ability to convey emotions, intentions, and sometimes even lies, without saying a single word. Whether it's a fleeting glance, a prolonged stare, or a subtle shift in direction, our eyes are constantly sending messages that reveal the truth about what we're feeling or thinking.

If you've ever been in a conversation where someone looked away when they spoke, or conversely, stared at you for too long, you probably felt something shift. Eyes can make us feel understood, comforted, or even manipulated. In fact, the way we use our eyes in communication plays a massive role in determining how honest and trustworthy we appear. A lack of eye contact often signals discomfort or deceit, while steady, open eye contact can suggest confidence and sincerity.

However, not all eye movements are the same. The way someone looks at you can tell you much more than just whether they're interested in what you're saying. The direction of their gaze, how often they blink, and whether they avoid eye contact can all be subtle indicators of their emotions, state of mind, and sometimes, their attempts to hide the truth. Understanding these signals is like learning a second language—a language where the eyes become the key to unlocking what someone is really trying to say.

What's even more fascinating is how manipulators use eye contact strategically. In social situations, people will often alter their eye movements to take control of the conversation or influence others' perceptions. From creating intimidation to making someone feel small, eye contact can be a tool for control. In this chapter, we'll dive into the different ways eye movements can reveal someone's truth and how skilled manipulators use eye contact to steer interactions in their favor. You'll learn how to recognize these patterns and decode the hidden meanings behind the gaze of those around you.

What Different Eye Movements Can Tell You About Someone's Truth

A few months ago, I was helping my friend Daniella prepare for an important job interview. Daniella had the experience and qualifications for the role, but like most people, she was feeling a little nervous. During our practice session, she seemed confident at first, but I noticed something that caught my attention. Every time we discussed her weaknesses or challenges in previous roles, her eyes began to move in a specific pattern. They would shift to the right, then briefly glance down before returning to focus on me. It wasn't just a nervous habit; her eye movements were telling me something important.

I didn't say anything at first, but after a few more questions, it became clear. When she was discussing areas of her past work where she wasn't entirely confident, her eyes weren't aligned with her words. In those moments, her eyes would flicker away, signaling discomfort and uncertainty. Daniella's body was betraying her. Her words said one thing, but her eyes told me something else. She was hiding her unease and trying to project confidence, but her eyes were revealing her true feelings of hesitation. This made me realize just how much we can learn about someone's inner state by paying attention to eye movements.

The eyes are incredibly powerful when it comes to non-verbal communication. Whether we're aware of it or not, our eyes reveal a lot about what's going on inside our minds. In Daniella's case, her eye movements were a clear indicator that she wasn't entirely at ease with her own answers, even though she was trying to appear calm and confident.

Let's break down what different eye movements can tell you about a person's thoughts, emotions, and possible deception:

- **Looking Upward:**

If someone looks upward, especially to the right, they are likely visualizing or recalling something they've seen before. However, if someone looks up to the left, they are typically creating or fabricating something, suggesting they might be lying or making up a story. When Daniella was asked about specific situations where she had to handle demanding clients, her eyes drifted upward to the left, indicating she was recalling a situation that wasn't entirely accurate.

- **Looking Down:**

When a person looks down, it can suggest guilt, shame, or discomfort. It's often an unconscious attempt to hide from a topic that makes them feel vulnerable. Daniella would usually look down when we talked about her past performance reviews. This subtle gesture indicated that she was uncomfortable discussing the negative feedback, even though she was trying to brush it off with confident answers. Looking down can also signal withdrawal or an attempt to retreat emotionally from a topic.

- **Avoiding Eye Contact:**

A key sign that someone may not be entirely truthful is when they avoid direct eye contact. If someone is uncomfortable, they may feel exposed, and this leads them to look away. When Daniella started talking about the challenges she faced with her previous manager, she looked away several times. This was a sign that she was either uncomfortable discussing the situation or possibly withholding some of the truth. Avoiding eye contact can suggest a lack of confidence in what someone is saying or a desire to hide emotions.

- **Excessive Eye Contact:**

On the other hand, when someone holds eye contact too intensely, it can be an attempt to dominate the conversation or create an impression of trustworthiness. Some people use prolonged eye contact to manipulate others or establish control. In Daniella's case, she didn't use this tactic, but if she had been trying to convince me of something, maintaining intense eye contact might have made me feel more pressured or inclined to believe her.

- **Rapid Blinking:**

Increased blinking is often a sign of nervousness, especially when someone is under pressure or feeling anxious. When we lie, our brains are working overtime, and this can cause physical responses like blinking faster than usual. In some cases, people who are uncomfortable may also blink more often to help relieve the tension. During the most challenging parts of Daniella's practice interview, I noticed her blinking slightly faster when she answered questions about her previous job. This was a subtle sign that she was a bit nervous, even though her answers sounded confident.

- **Pupillary Dilation:**

The size of our pupils can give us important clues about our emotional state. When we are interested, excited, or engaged, our pupils dilate, becoming larger. This reaction happens automatically and is linked to positive emotions or heightened attention. Conversely, constricted pupils could indicate discomfort, irritation, or negative feelings. While discussing the aspects of her new job that she was excited about, Daniella's pupils were slightly dilated, suggesting genuine interest. But when we touched on the areas she found more challenging, her pupils appeared to constrict, indicating discomfort.

- **Looking Around:**

Looking around the room, especially when someone is being questioned or discussing a sensitive topic, can signal evasiveness. If a person's eyes dart around or if they glance at the exit, it could suggest they're trying to avoid the subject or disengage from the conversation. Daniella did this when I pressed her on specific aspects of her career, especially areas where she felt less confident. This movement showed that she wasn't entirely comfortable with the conversation and was subconsciously trying to escape it.

- **Slow Blinking:**

Slow, deliberate blinking typically indicates calmness, thoughtfulness, or genuine engagement. When someone is interested in the conversation and at ease, their blinking slows down. In Daniella's case, when she spoke about her passion for the industry and her long-term goals, her blinking became slower, showing that she was emotionally invested in the topic. It was a sign of authenticity and comfort.

The eyes can be incredibly revealing, offering a window into someone's true thoughts and feelings. While words may attempt to cover up the truth, eye movements often give us away. Paying attention to these subtle signals can help you understand what someone is really thinking, whether they're being truthful or hiding something.

How Manipulators Use Eye Contact to Control Conversations

Eye contact is more than just a way to show you're listening. It's a tool that can be used to influence, control, and even manipulate the direction of a conversation. Manipulators are experts at using their gaze to create a sense of power, manipulate your emotions, and make you feel a certain way without saying a word. Eye contact, when used skillfully, can make you feel more comfortable, uncomfortable, intimidated, or even powerless, all depending on how it's applied. Let's break down how this works.

Intense Staring is one of the most common tactics manipulators use to control a conversation. Have you ever been in a conversation where someone stares at you for too long, making you feel uncomfortable or pressured to speak? This is done deliberately. The manipulator locks eyes with you, refusing to look away, creating a feeling of intimidation. It's a power move. The longer they stare, the more you feel like you're under scrutiny. The goal is to make you feel uncomfortable and vulnerable, so you end up agreeing with what they say or backing down from your point. The discomfort you feel can cause you to soften your stance, making it easier for them to take control of the situation.

Another common strategy is avoidance of eye contact. When someone won't look at you while you're talking, it can feel like they're dismissing you or not interested in what you're saying. A manipulator might do this deliberately to make you feel as if you have to work harder to gain their attention or approval. This shift in gaze can leave you feeling frustrated or like you're being ignored, creating a power imbalance. By not making eye contact, the manipulator forces you to seek their approval or to become more eager in your attempts to engage them.

Some manipulators are more subtle in their approach and use eye contact to create confusion. They might look away quickly, look in different directions, or even glance around the room while you're talking. This can make you feel as if you're not the priority in the conversation or that the manipulator is distracted by something else. This subtle shift can cause self-doubt. You might begin wondering if you're saying the right things or if they're losing interest in you. It's a tactic to keep you unsure of where you stand and to make you feel off-balance.

There's also the manipulator who uses quick glances to make you feel like you're constantly under evaluation. Instead of looking at you fully, they give you short, sharp glances as if they're assessing you or your statements. This constant motion of their eyes makes you feel as though you're being judged or that you're not fully in control of the conversation. It can be challenging to know where you stand, and this constant assessment can lead you to second-guess yourself and give the manipulator more power.

One of the more advanced techniques involves holding eye contact too long. In everyday conversations, eye contact naturally shifts as we speak, breaking and re-establishing. However, a manipulator may maintain steady eye contact for longer than they feel comfortable. This prolonged stare can make the other person feel trapped in the conversation, as though they cannot break free from the intensity of the gaze. It's a tactic used to make the other person feel powerless. The goal is to overwhelm you with the intensity of their focus, making it harder to hold your ground in the conversation.

There's also the strategic use of blinking. When manipulators want to come across as calm or authoritative, they may blink slowly. This can create an aura of control. If they're trying to intimidate or assert dominance, they might deliberately slow their blinking to appear more collected. On the flip side, if someone is blinking rapidly or excessively, it's often a sign of anxiety. In manipulative conversations, rapid blinking can be used as a way to signal stress while simultaneously trying to conceal it. A manipulator might use this technique to draw attention to their perceived vulnerability and get others to sympathize with them, thereby shifting the power dynamic in their favor.

Breaking eye contact strategically is another manipulation technique. A manipulator might hold your gaze for just long enough to make you feel unsettled, then suddenly look away at key moments. This break in eye contact causes confusion, leaving you uncertain about the status of the conversation. By switching between engaging and avoiding eye contact, they keep you on your toes, making you more likely to second-guess your words and agree with their position.

The key to spotting these manipulative tactics is paying attention to patterns in their eye contact. A person who is confident in a conversation will use eye contact to engage with you, match your rhythm, and show genuine interest. Manipulators, however, use eye contact strategically to influence you, make you feel uncomfortable, or assert power in the conversation.

Once you begin to notice these shifts in eye contact, you can better recognize when someone is trying to take control. Whether it's through prolonged staring, quick glances, or breaking eye contact, these subtle cues reveal more than you might realize. Learning to spot these signals will give you the ability to navigate conversations more confidently, without falling victim to manipulation.

Key Takeaways:

- Eye contact reveals emotions: Eye movements can show if someone is uncomfortable, anxious, or confident. Whether they avoid your gaze or maintain intense eye contact, these cues help reveal their true feelings and intentions during conversations.

- Manipulators use eye contact strategically: Skilled manipulators control conversations through eye contact. By using prolonged stares, avoiding eye contact, or breaking eye contact at key moments, they can create discomfort and dominate the power dynamic in a conversation.

- Patterns of eye contact signal control: A person's eye movements often follow a pattern, and recognizing these patterns can reveal when someone is trying to influence or manipulate you. Subtle shifts in their gaze can show underlying intentions.

In this chapter, we explored how eye contact can give away someone's emotions and intentions, mainly when used to manipulate.

Now that we understand how eye contact can shape power dynamics and reveal hidden truths, we can get deeper into how emotional manipulation plays a significant role in controlling others. From guilt to fear, emotional manipulation can subtly push people to act in ways they wouldn't usually choose. Let's explore how manipulators play with feelings and how to recognize these tactics in real-time.

Chapter 6:

Emotional Manipulation: The Art of Playing with Feelings

You know that feeling when someone pulls out the "I did this for you, and now you owe me" card? It's like emotional debt, but without the receipt. Welcome to the world of emotional manipulation! It's where feelings become the currency, and the goal is to get you to do something, whether you want to or not, by playing with your emotions. You might have already encountered these tactics in the form of guilt trips, guilt-inducing "heartfelt" pleas, or those well-timed "you're the only one who can help me" moments. You know the ones I'm talking about.

Manipulators are masters at this game. They know how to push your buttons in just the right way, making you feel responsible for their emotions. Want to feel guilty? They've got it covered. Feeling afraid? Oh, they'll work that too. It's all about hitting the emotional sweet spots that make you feel a sense of urgency or obligation. Whether it's guilt, fear, or sympathy, manipulators know precisely how to tap into your feelings and use them against you.

The tricky part is that these emotional tactics are often so subtle. At first, you might feel genuinely compassionate and want to help, but after a few rounds of these emotional curveballs, you start to realise you've been played. Recognising emotional manipulation is all about seeing through the emotional fog and spotting the patterns. Trust me, once you know what to look for, it's like you've got a superpower.

In this chapter, we'll break down the psychological tricks manipulators use to twist your feelings and how to recognise when someone is trying to manipulate you emotionally. Spoiler alert: It's not always as straightforward as it seems! Let's get in and learn how to spot the subtle art of playing with emotions.

The Psychological Tactics of Guilt, Fear, and Sympathy

Did you know that about 80% of people feel manipulated emotionally in some way in their daily lives, whether in relationships, at work, or even with friends? This statistic highlights how common emotional manipulation really is. It's one of the trickiest forms of control because it's often so subtle. The key emotions manipulators target are guilt, fear, and sympathy. These emotions can be powerful tools to control how others behave and react. Understanding how these tactics work is essential to protecting yourself from falling victim to them. Let's take a deeper look at how these psychological tactics play out in real life.

Guilt is one of the most potent emotions used by manipulators. We all experience guilt when we feel like we've done something wrong or failed to meet someone's expectations. A manipulator will use this emotion to make you feel responsible for their feelings or actions. Have you ever heard someone say, "I can't believe you didn't help me with this, after everything I've done for you?" That's a guilt-tripping tactic. The manipulator is making you feel like you owe them something, even when you don't.

They might not say it directly, but by pushing this feeling of guilt, they create an emotional debt that you feel the need to pay back. For example, a friend might say, "You didn't call me when I was sick. I thought you were my best friend." This statement is designed to make you feel bad for not meeting their expectation, even if you had a good reason for not being able to help. Over time, if a manipulator keeps using this guilt tactic, it can make you feel constantly obligated to meet their needs, whether you have the time or energy to do so.

Fear is another powerful tool manipulators use to control others. Fear of rejection, fear of failure, or even fear of missing out are all emotions that manipulators will prey on. A manipulator might create a sense of urgency or pressure to make you act quickly, often without considering your own needs. For example, a colleague might say, "If you don't finish this project today, it's going to be a disaster. Everyone will be angry at you." By creating this false sense of urgency, the manipulator is making you fearful of the consequences, even though the situation might not be as dire as it seems.

The fear of disappointing someone is another common manipulation tactic. They will create a situation where you feel like you're responsible for their happiness or success. If they can make you afraid that your actions—or lack thereof—will negatively affect them, you're more likely to say yes to whatever they want. A partner might say, "If you don't do this for me, it'll mean you don't love me." This type of manipulation plays on the fear of rejection or abandonment, making you feel responsible for someone else's emotional well-being.

Sympathy is the third emotion manipulator that the manipulator often uses to control others. We all feel sympathy for others, especially when they are going through a tough time. A manipulator knows how to exploit this emotion by making you feel so sorry for their situation that you're willing to do anything to help, even if it's something you're not comfortable with. For example, a friend might say, "I don't know what I would do without you. I'm going through such a tough time right now." The manipulator is using their situation to make you feel like you must help them, even if it's at the expense of your own well-being.

Sometimes, manipulators will share just enough of their personal struggles to make you feel needed, without revealing the whole picture. They might make it seem like they have no one else to turn to, subtly making you feel like you're their only hope. This can cause you to overextend yourself, offering help or support when you're already stretched thin. Over time, this can become an emotional burden, as you find yourself constantly giving without receiving much in return.

These three emotional manipulation tactics—guilt, fear, and sympathy—are used to create a sense of obligation in the other person. They tap into our natural desire to help, to feel good about ourselves, and to maintain harmony in relationships. The tricky part is that these tactics are often not obvious. Manipulators don't come right out and say, "I want you to feel guilty, so you'll do what I want." Instead, they use subtle psychological tricks to make you feel like you're doing the right thing when, in reality, they are just taking advantage of your emotions to control you.

The first step in recognising emotional manipulation is awareness. If you start noticing that someone is using guilt, fear, or sympathy to control your decisions, it's time to step back and reassess the situation. Ask yourself, "Am I doing this because I genuinely want to, or am I doing it out of pressure?" By learning to recognise these signs, you can stop being manipulated by emotional tactics and begin to set healthy boundaries that protect your emotional well-being.

Recognising Emotional Manipulation in Real Time

Emotional manipulation is everywhere, and most of us are so used to it that we don't even notice it happening anymore. It's not just the obvious stuff like a partner guilt-tripping you or a boss throwing a pity party to get you to stay late. Emotional manipulation happens in the little moments, the ones that seem so harmless but are actually designed to get you to do something you don't want to do. The truth is, you're probably being emotionally manipulated right now, and you don't even know it. And here's the kicker: most people don't even realise they're doing it.

The world runs on emotions. Manipulators understand this better than anyone. They know how to push buttons, twist feelings, and use guilt, fear, and sympathy to get you to act in ways that serve their needs. The worst part? They make you feel like it's your choice. You think you're being a good person, that you're doing the right thing. You might even believe you are the one at fault when, in reality, someone else has been using your emotions to control the situation. If you don't recognise this, you're trapped in their game. It's time to break the cycle.

If you're constantly feeling guilty for not doing enough, not saying yes, or not meeting someone's needs, chances are you've been manipulated. People who play the guilt card are experts at making you feel like a bad person. They love to say things like, "I can't believe you'd let me down like this," or, "I thought you cared about me." If you've heard those words and felt the weight of emotional responsibility, you've just experienced emotional manipulation. The person isn't asking for help—they're making you feel like you owe it to them, as if your worth as a friend, partner, or colleague is tied to how much you give, sacrifice, or apologise for not being perfect.

Emotional manipulators are using guilt as a weapon to get you to take responsibility for their emotional state. When someone tells you they're upset because you didn't do something for them, they're not actually asking you to solve their problem. What they're really asking is for you to carry their emotional burden and make it your responsibility. You're not just helping—you're saving them from their emotions.

Recognising fear-based manipulation is just as important, but this one is trickier. People love to use fear to get others to act. Don't believe me? Look at every single ad that plays on FOMO (fear of missing out) or impending doom. Fear is a brilliant way to manipulate others into making decisions quickly, without thinking. A common fear tactic is saying something like, "If you don't do this now, everything could fall apart," or "This could be your last chance. If you miss it, you'll regret it forever." That's a direct manipulation of your anxiety.

It's the same with the person who tells you, "If you don't help me, I'll be so upset. I don't know if I can trust you again if you don't do this for me." They've just created a scenario where you're the one at fault if they experience negative emotions. You think it's your job to fix things, to prevent a disaster, to stop them from feeling bad. Guess what? It's not.

The worst part is, you often agree to these fear-based demands. You might not even realise that you're giving up your own needs in the process. You're acting on fear of what will happen to the relationship or situation, instead of acting on what you truly want or need. You're walking on eggshells to avoid making them upset or disappointing them. The moment you do that, you're no longer in control of your life.

Sympathy manipulation works similarly. The person who's always telling you how hard their life is or how much they've suffered loves to manipulate your empathy. "I've been through so much," they might say. "I don't know how much more I can take." They look to you for sympathy, and they expect you to feel sorry for them, then step in and take care of their problems. Here's the twist— they don't want help. They want validation and attention, and they're using your good heart to get it. If you feel like you're always the one being asked to solve other people's problems while you're struggling with your own, you're likely being manipulated.

Sympathy manipulation is tricky because it tugs at our natural desire to help others. We're taught to be compassionate, but we're rarely trained to recognise when someone is using our sympathy against us. They pull at your heartstrings and make you feel like you're the only one who can "save" them. Guess what? You're not responsible for anyone else's emotional state. You don't have to carry the weight of their emotions, their struggles, or their poor decisions. You don't have to be the saviour in every situation.

Recognising emotional manipulation in real time takes practice, but it's critical if you want to stop being controlled. Trust your gut. If something feels off—if you feel drained, anxious, or guilty after a conversation, it's a sign you've been manipulated. Emotional manipulators rely on you second-guessing yourself. They want you to feel responsible for their feelings, and they want you to question whether you're doing enough. When you can recognise the signs—guilt, fear, sympathy—you can start to set boundaries.

Stop apologising for things that aren't your fault. Stop saying yes when you mean no. Stop letting people control your emotions with their guilt, fear, or sob stories. Emotional manipulation is about control, but once you recognise it, you take back that control. You don't have to fix other people's problems or carry their emotional weight. The key is learning how to protect your own emotional well-being and put your needs first. Only then can you have genuine, healthy relationships that don't leave you feeling drained or used.

Key Takeaways:

- **Emotional manipulation uses guilt, fear, and sympathy:** Manipulators exploit these emotions to control others. They make you feel responsible for their feelings or fears, pushing you to act against your best interests for their benefit.

- **Recognising emotional manipulation is crucial for self-protection:** Manipulation often feels subtle and natural, but once you recognise guilt-tripping, fear tactics, and sympathy manipulation, you can set boundaries and avoid being emotionally controlled by others' agendas.

- **Healthy relationships require emotional boundaries:** Emotional manipulators thrive on your willingness to prioritise their feelings over your own. Setting boundaries helps you maintain control over your emotions and prevents you from being taken advantage of in any relationship.

This chapter highlighted how emotional manipulators use guilt, fear, and sympathy to control others. Understanding these tactics is the first step in recognising when they're being used on you. The next step is to learn how to communicate effectively while maintaining your boundaries.

Persuasion is a powerful tool, but it can be used for both good and bad purposes. Let's explore the psychology behind persuasive communication, how to use persuasion ethically, and how to spot when someone is using persuasion unethically. Ready to sharpen your skills? Let's get into the art of persuasion.

Chapter 7:

The Subtle Art of Persuasion

I remember the time I bought a fancy new coffee maker. It wasn't something I had planned on buying, but there I was, credit card in hand, standing in the store ready to make the purchase.

What happened? A well-timed conversation with a salesperson, of course. He didn't pressure me or tell me I "had to" buy it. Instead, he asked me a few questions about my morning routine, how I felt about my current coffee setup, and if I was looking to "level up" my mornings. The next thing I knew, I was considering how much better my life could be with a fancy coffee machine. I walked out of that store with the exact model he suggested, thinking I had made the decision all on my own.

Looking back, I realised I had just been persuaded. He didn't "sell" me. He guided me into seeing how owning that coffee maker would solve my problems. He didn't use flashy sales tactics or push me to buy it; he used a subtle and straightforward approach that made me believe it was my idea. That moment stuck with me because it was a perfect example of how powerful persuasion can be when done correctly. It's not about being manipulative or forceful. It's about subtly shaping someone's thought process in a way that feels natural and even empowering.

This interaction didn't make me feel like I had been tricked or taken advantage of. In fact, I felt good about my decision. That's the key to ethical persuasion: it makes everyone feel like they've made the right choice without feeling coerced. In this chapter, we're going to dig into the psychology behind persuasion, how it works when it's done ethically, and how you can spot when someone is using it unethically to get what they want.

The Psychology Behind Persuasive Communication

The human mind is fascinating in how it processes information, reacts to emotions, and makes decisions. Understanding the psychology behind persuasion requires understanding how the brain works when it's absorbing, evaluating, and responding to information.

The truth is, we don't always make decisions based on logic. The brain loves shortcuts and relies heavily on biases, emotions, and past experiences. These shortcuts, or heuristics, make us quicker in making decisions but leave us vulnerable to persuasion. Let's break down how the brain works in the context of persuasion, and why these psychological processes make us so susceptible to persuasion techniques.

First, the brain seeks **certainty**. Humans crave certainty in a world full of unknowns. Our brains work to eliminate doubt and anxiety by making quick decisions. Persuaders use this need for certainty to their advantage by presenting information in a clear, simple way that helps the mind feel safe.

If the information is easy to digest and appears reliable, the brain is more likely to accept it. This is why ads, presentations, or persuasive arguments often focus on providing straightforward, clear information that eliminates confusion. The brain rewards clarity and certainty with a release of dopamine, making the decision seem more agreeable and rewarding.

The second key element in persuasive psychology is **cognitive dissonance**. This is the mental discomfort we experience when our actions and beliefs don't align. We're often motivated to reduce this discomfort, either by changing our behaviour or altering our beliefs. For persuaders, this is a powerful tool. If you can get someone to admit that their current behaviour doesn't align with their values or goals, you've created the perfect opening for persuasion.

For example, if you're trying to convince someone to stop procrastinating, you might first ask them how they feel about wasting time. Once they express discomfort or guilt, you can present a solution that feels aligned with their values, thereby reducing their cognitive dissonance. The brain naturally seeks consistency, so when faced with a choice that aligns with their beliefs, people are more likely to say yes.

Another important psychological principle is the **emotion-driven decision-making process.** People often believe they make decisions based on logic, but emotions are the proper drivers. Think about how you make choices at the store. If a product makes you feel happy, comfortable, or excited, you are more likely to buy it, even if there is a similar option available that's cheaper or more practical.

The brain is deeply emotional, and when emotions are activated, they can often override logic. This is why persuasive communication focuses heavily on emotions. Positive emotions like excitement, hope, or trust can make someone more likely to say yes to an idea, product, or proposal. It's not about facts and logic—it's about how the message makes the person feel.

Reciprocity is another powerful psychological principle in persuasion. People feel a natural obligation to return favours. If someone does something for you, even something small, you are more likely to do something in return. This principle is used by salespeople, marketers, and anyone trying to persuade others.

They might offer a free sample, a compliment, or even a small favour to trigger the feeling of obligation. The brain processes this as a form of "social debt," where you feel the need to reciprocate to balance the relationship. This is why you often feel more inclined to buy something after getting a free trial or product sample. The idea of returning the favour has subconsciously influenced your brain.

Commitment and consistency also play a massive role in how persuasion works. Once you commit, even a small one, your brain wants to stay consistent with that commitment. This is why someone who agrees to a small request is more likely to agree to a larger request later. For example, if you agree to a salesperson's request for a quick survey, you're more likely to buy the product they pitch to you afterwards. The brain dislikes inconsistency and will work hard to align behaviour with previously made commitments. This is why persuasion tactics often start small, with seemingly innocent requests that set the stage for larger asks.

Another psychological factor at play in persuasion is the need for **social validation**. The brain is wired to look to others for cues about what is correct or acceptable. If we see other people doing something, we're more likely to do it too. This is called social proof, and it's why reviews, testimonials, and influencer endorsements are so powerful. The brain processes social cues as signals of safety, helping us decide what to do. People feel more comfortable with a decision if they see others making the same choice. Persuaders use social proof to reassure people that their decision is a safe one, making it easier for them to take action. If everyone else is doing it, the brain reasons, it must be okay.

Persuasion also heavily relies on the brain's processing of information overload. People are bombarded with information constantly, and the brain can't process it all. As a result, it looks for shortcuts, trusting authority figures or familiar brands.

This is why you might trust a well-known brand over a new one, even if the new one offers a better deal. Your brain's reliance on familiarity and trust makes it easier for those who hold authority or have established credibility to persuade others. When someone presents themselves as an expert or a trusted source, the brain tends to accept their claims without much resistance.

Finally, the brain's **need for control** plays into persuasion. People want to feel like they are making decisions on their own, even when they are being influenced. This is why many persuasive strategies focus on making someone feel like they are in control of their choice. When you feel empowered to make a decision, your brain is more likely to feel comfortable with it. Persuasion isn't about pushing people into a corner; it's about guiding them to a conclusion where they think they are the ones making the choice.

Understanding how the brain works in the context of persuasion opens up a whole new world of opportunities. When you can tap into these psychological principles, you're not just persuading someone; you're guiding their mind to make the decision you want naturally. It's not about manipulation; it's about understanding how people think and using that knowledge to lead them in a way that benefits everyone.

How to Use Persuasion Ethically (And Spot the Unethical Tactics)

Persuasion can be compelling when used for good. It can help you sell a product, convince someone of a better idea, or motivate someone to take action. The key is to use it ethically. Ethical persuasion is about influencing others in a way that respects their autonomy, encourages positive outcomes, and maintains their trust.

It's about guiding people to make decisions that are in their best interest without manipulating or deceiving them. Here's how you can use persuasion ethically while also spotting when someone is using unethical tactics to manipulate you.

Ethical Persuasion: The Key Principles

- **Focus on mutual benefit:**

When you persuade someone, always remember that the decision should benefit both parties. Whether you're convincing a friend to try a new restaurant or pitching a business idea, the end goal should be win-win. Ethical persuasion leads to outcomes that leave everyone feeling good about the decision without anyone feeling manipulated or coerced.

- **Be transparent:**

Honesty is a cornerstone of ethical persuasion. Never hide important information or mislead others to get your way. If you're trying to convince someone of a product's value, make sure you share all the pros and cons. Transparency builds trust, and when trust is built, persuasion becomes a natural and easy process.

- **Respect autonomy:**

Ethical persuasion always respects a person's ability to make their own decision. Don't try to make someone feel like they have no choice or that your idea is the only option. Allow them to make their own decision based on the information you provide. Persuasion is about guiding someone's thinking, not forcing them into it. Empowerment is the goal, not control.

- **Appeal to emotions ethically:**

You can use emotions to persuade, but only in a way that's genuine and positive. Emotional appeals can be incredibly effective when used in the right way. For example, you can tell a heartwarming story that resonates with someone's values or use humour to connect with them. Just make sure the emotions you tap into aren't being used to exploit or manipulate. Empathy should guide your approach, not fear or guilt.

- **Provide value:**

Always ensure that your persuasive efforts are aimed at offering value if you're trying to persuade someone to take action; show them how it's going to benefit them. Whether it's in a professional or personal setting, people are more likely to say yes when they can see the value in your request. For example, instead of just trying to sell a product, show how it makes their life easier or helps them solve a problem.

- **Be patient and give time:**

Ethical persuasion doesn't rush. You don't need to pressure anyone into making a decision right away. Give people the space to think things through. When someone feels rushed, they are more likely to make an emotional decision rather than a rational one. If your offer is as great as you say, they'll come around to it with time.

Recognising Unethical Persuasion

Sometimes, people try to use persuasion unethically. It might seem persuasive at first, but there's a darker side to it. Here are the signs that you're being manipulated:

- **Pressuring for immediate decisions:**

If someone pressures you into making a decision right now, without giving you time to think, there's a good chance you're being manipulated. Unethical persuaders often create a false sense of urgency to get you to act without considering your best interests. They might use phrases like "You must decide now" or "This offer won't last long" to rush you into a quick decision. A genuine, ethical offer would allow you time to reflect on it.

- **Using guilt to push you:**

When someone makes you feel guilty for not agreeing to their proposal, they're crossing the line into manipulation. For example, if someone says, "I've done so much for you, it's the least you could do for me," they're trying to make you feel responsible for their emotional state. Guilt is a powerful tool, and when used unethically, it can force people to make decisions they wouldn't otherwise make. Guilt-tripping is one of the easiest manipulative tactics to spot.

- **Concealing important details:**

If someone is presenting you with information and leaving out key details, that's an immediate red flag. Withholding information or failing to disclose potential risks is a sure sign of unethical persuasion. For example, if a salesperson doesn't tell you about the hidden fees on a product until after you've committed to buying it, they've used deceit to manipulate you into making a decision.

- **Using emotional blackmail:**

Emotional blackmail is a form of manipulation where the persuader threatens to withdraw affection, approval, or even basic respect unless you comply with their wishes. This could be something as simple as "If you loved me, you'd do this for me," or "If you really care about the team, you'll do this." They are using manipulative guilt and fear to control your actions.

- **Exaggerating claims:**

Manipulating through exaggerated claims is unethical persuasion. If someone promises something that seems too good to be true or overstates the benefits of something, they are pushing you toward a decision that isn't fully informed. For instance, if someone claims a product will solve all your problems without offering clear evidence or context, they are making exaggerated promises. Ethical persuasion always includes realistic expectations and doesn't deceive or inflate the truth.

- **Appealing to fear or insecurity:**

Some persuaders exploit your fears or insecurities to get you to act. For example, they might say, "If you don't do this now, you'll regret it forever," or "You're running out of time to fix this." Fear is a very effective tactic, but it's also one of the most unethical. When persuasion focuses on creating anxiety or fear, it forces the person to act out of distress rather than reason. This is a clear attempt at coercion rather than ethical persuasion.

How to Avoid Manipulation

- **Trust your gut:**

If something feels off or you feel pressured, take a step back and think it through. Gut feelings are often our brains telling us something isn't right.

- **Ask for time to think:**

Give yourself space to process. An ethical persuader will respect your need for time to reflect, while a manipulator will try to rush you.

- **Set clear boundaries:**

Don't be afraid to say "no" or ask questions if you feel uncomfortable. People who use ethical persuasion will respect your boundaries; manipulators will try to cross them.

In conclusion, persuasion is a powerful tool that can lead to positive outcomes if used ethically. Always focus on providing value, respecting the other person's autonomy, and building trust. Recognise when you're being manipulated and stay aware of your emotional triggers. The best persuaders are those who guide others to a decision without pressure or deceit, using psychology to help, not to control.

Key Takeaways:

- **Ethical persuasion focuses on mutual benefit:** Persuasion works best when both parties benefit. Ethical persuasion seeks to guide others towards decisions that improve their lives while respecting their autonomy and desires, ensuring that everyone involved feels valued and respected.

- **Understanding psychological principles enhances persuasion:** Tapping into how the brain processes emotions, seeks certainty, and responds to social cues allows you to persuade others ethically. It's not about manipulation; it's about aligning their thinking with their best interests.

- **Unethical tactics rely on guilt, fear, and pressure:** Manipulators use emotional triggers to control and influence decisions. By recognising signs of guilt-tripping, fear-based tactics, and exaggerated claims, you can avoid being manipulated and ensure that persuasion remains respectful and fair.

In this chapter, we've explored how ethical persuasion works and how to spot when someone is engaging in unethical manipulation.

Now that we've covered the psychology behind persuading with integrity, let's move on to another powerful communication tool—**silence**. It's often overlooked, but silence can hold more power than words. We'll see how manipulators use it to create tension and control conversations. Are you ready to unlock the hidden potential of silence? Then keep reading.

Chapter 8:

Does Silence Speak Louder Than Words?

When I think about the power of silence, I think back to my childhood and a teacher I had in primary school. Her name was Mrs. Lawson, and she had a way of controlling an entire classroom without raising her voice. Most teachers relied on shouting, clapping, or scolding to keep order, but not Mrs. Lawson. She had something more effective: she used silence.

I still remember one particular afternoon. The classroom was noisy, kids were throwing paper balls, chairs scraped across the floor, and it felt like chaos. Suddenly, Mrs. Lawson stopped speaking. She just stood at the front of the class, arms folded, and looked at us with calm patience.

The silence was so thick that it felt like the air itself had become heavier. At first, we didn't notice, but slowly, one by one, heads turned, and voices faded until the room went completely quiet. She hadn't said a word, but somehow, she had everyone's full attention. What made it more powerful was that the silence wasn't angry or threatening. It was controlled and deliberate, and it made us realize that we were the ones in the wrong.

That moment taught me that silence is not empty; it can carry weight, create tension, and shift power in any interaction. Mrs. Lawson wasn't manipulating us out of cruelty, but she understood how silence could be used to steer behavior without raising her tone. It left a stronger impression than if she had shouted, and it made us respect her authority more deeply.

As I grew older, I noticed this same tactic in different situations, from conversations at home to meetings at work. People who know how to wield silence often control the flow of communication, while those who feel uncomfortable with silence rush to fill it, giving away more than they intended. In this chapter, we'll explore how manipulators use silence to gain control and why the absence of words often speaks louder than the words themselves.

How Manipulators Use Silence to Create Tension and Gain Control

Silence can be like the pause before the storm. It's a quiet that holds all the energy of a thunderclap, waiting to explode. It's the space between words where meaning shifts, where discomfort brews, and where the power dynamics of any conversation can change without a single word being said. In many ways, silence is one of the most potent tools manipulators use to control conversations, create tension, and gain influence.

Let's start with a simple analogy. Imagine you're playing a game of chess. The game's rhythm depends on the moves made by each player. Each move has a purpose, and each time you move, you expect a response. Now imagine, for a moment, your opponent stops moving. No new pieces are played, no adjustments are made. Silence fills the board. You sit there, wondering if your opponent is about to strike with a brilliant move, or if they're waiting for you to make the first mistake. The tension builds, and you feel the pressure of making the right move, not just to win the game, but to avoid the discomfort of sitting in uncertainty.

This is precisely how silence works in conversations. When a manipulator chooses to remain silent, it creates a gap in the conversation—a moment that seems filled with unspoken weight. People are not comfortable with silence. We are social creatures, wired to fill the quiet with words, explanations, and actions. When that silence lingers, our brains naturally feel the need to fill it. It's in these moments of silence that manipulators gain control.

Manipulators understand this psychological reaction. They know that if they leave a pause in a conversation long enough, you will fill it, often saying more than you intended. This is a trick they use to get you to divulge information, make decisions you might not be ready for, or even backtrack on something you previously said. The longer the silence, the more pressure you feel to break it. This pressure can make you uncomfortable—and when people are uncomfortable, they're much more likely to act impulsively or go along with things to avoid that discomfort.

Consider a conversation with someone who's skilled at using silence to their advantage. They might ask you a question, and instead of rushing to respond, they sit back and wait. You can feel their gaze on you, their expectation hanging in the air, and the weight of their silence starts to feel like a demand. The moment stretches, your mind races, and you feel the need to respond, to fill the silence, to make the tension go away. In your attempt to break the silence, you might find yourself saying things you hadn't planned to say, offering more details than you intended, or even agreeing to something out of sheer discomfort.

This is manipulation in action—a quiet power move. The manipulator knows precisely how to control the flow of the conversation by allowing silence to sit in the space between them and you. They don't need to force an answer out of you. The pressure of the quiet does it for them.

Another way silence works as a tool for manipulators is by creating uncertainty. When someone withholds information or refuses to answer a question directly, the silence that follows can lead you to make assumptions. Your brain wants clarity, so it starts to fill in the blanks, often with the worst-case scenario. This is when the manipulator has you exactly where they want you: in a state of unease, uncertainty, and doubt. The more you try to fill the silence with your own assumptions, the more you begin to distort the truth in your mind. The manipulator, meanwhile, remains silent, letting your mind spin out of control.

The silence creates a psychological gap between what's being said and what's left unsaid. This gap is often where manipulative power lies. The brain is forced to interpret the silence, and in doing so, you start projecting your own emotions, concerns, and assumptions onto the situation. The manipulator doesn't need to tell you what's on their mind; they need to leave enough space for you to fill it with your own thoughts.

Silence is also an incredibly effective tool in creating emotional tension. A manipulator may use silence in moments of anger, disappointment, or judgment, forcing you to wonder what they're thinking. You can feel their emotional weight even though they haven't said a word. The discomfort of not knowing what they're feeling, whether they're upset, angry, or dissatisfied, often causes you to feel more anxious or guilty, even when you haven't done anything wrong. Manipulators frequently leverage this emotional tension to create an environment where you feel compelled to fix things, apologize, or change your behavior without them ever having to ask. The silence becomes a form of control, dictating the emotional atmosphere of the conversation.

It's easy to underestimate the power of silence because it's so subtle, so passive. However, the reality is that it's one of the most potent forms of non-verbal communication. Manipulators use it strategically to intimidate, confuse, and pressure others into making decisions or concessions that serve their agenda. The uncomfortable quiet isn't a void; it's filled with all the emotional and psychological weight that makes it so hard to break.

Recognizing when silence is being used to manipulate is crucial. If you feel an overwhelming urge to fill a silence, or if you find yourself offering up more information than you intended, take a step back and ask yourself why. Is the silence uncomfortable because you feel pressured or because you're trying to avoid tension? Manipulators know that we crave resolution, and silence is one of the most effective ways to create the discomfort that drives us to act.

The Hidden Power of Non-Verbal Communication in Silence

In 1961, a moment occurred that would go down in history as a perfect example of how silence can shape perceptions. It was during the first-ever televised presidential debate between John

F. Kennedy and Richard Nixon. This debate is often credited with changing the course of American politics, not because of what was said, but because of how silence and non-verbal communication played a pivotal role in shaping the outcome.

At the time, Nixon was considered the more experienced candidate. He had a long political career, serving as vice president and a senator. Kennedy, on the other hand, was relatively young and still building his political reputation. Nixon entered the debate with experience, but he was also battling an illness that had left him visibly exhausted. His appearance was less than ideal—he had a five o'clock shadow, he was sweating, and he fidgeted nervously throughout the debate. On the other hand, Kennedy, though younger, had the composure of someone much more seasoned. He appeared calm, collected, and in control.

What happened in that debate wasn't just a matter of who had the better arguments. It was about how each candidate's non-verbal communication conveyed authority, confidence, and trust. While Nixon was speaking, his body language told a very different story than his words. He leaned forward, his voice was strained, and he looked as though he was constantly trying to push through discomfort. Meanwhile, Kennedy's calm demeanor, unhurried movements, and deliberate pauses gave the impression of control. He didn't just speak; he allowed his words to sit in the air, giving silence the space it needed to shape the conversation.

Nixon, despite his strong arguments, couldn't escape the tension created by his discomfort. His body was telling a different story, and his attempts to fill that silence with words made it more obvious. Kennedy, on the other hand, used silence strategically. He wasn't afraid of a pause. When Nixon spoke, Kennedy often remained silent, letting his confidence and calm fill the room.

Those silences in the debate were more than just a break from words; they were a statement, a tool of communication that put Kennedy in control.

Here's the key lesson from that debate: Silence is not just the absence of sound; it is a powerful form of communication. When used intentionally, silence can speak louder than any words. It can shift the direction of a conversation, expose discomfort, or convey confidence. Manipulators understand this psychological power.

They know that silence can be used to control a situation, increase tension, or make the other person feel uncomfortable. In everyday life, this kind of silence often goes unnoticed. You might encounter a boss who says nothing after asking you a question, a friend who goes silent after you disagree, or a partner who uses silence as a tool to control an argument. These are not always coincidences. Silence can be carefully crafted to send a message without uttering a single word.

Manipulators use silence to create emotional tension. Think of how a conversation feels when one person doesn't respond right away. That pause often leaves the other person feeling uneasy, second-guessing themselves, or even trying harder to make their point. Silence in these moments can make you feel vulnerable. Your brain instinctively wants to fill the silence, often saying more than you intended in an attempt to resolve the discomfort. In a negotiation or an argument, when one person remains silent after you speak, it often leads to unwanted pressure that forces you to respond. It's the fear of the unknown; you don't know if they agree, if they're offended, or if they're just waiting for you to make the next move.

A classic example of this can be seen in many workplace environments. Have you ever been in a meeting where your boss asked you a direct question, then remained silent while staring at you? That silence makes you uncomfortable, doesn't it? Your brain starts scrambling for answers. You feel the need to fill the space, to break the silence, and often, that leads to saying something you didn't mean or over-explaining yourself. That moment of silence gives your boss control over the conversation without saying a word. It's an unspoken power that can manipulate the flow of communication.

Another way silence is used for control is by withholding information. In some situations, a manipulator will stay silent on specific points, leaving you to fill in the gaps. This silence can make you doubt yourself, question your decisions, or feel like you're missing something important. The silence keeps you on edge and makes you second-guess your understanding of the situation. This tactic is used to create uncertainty in the other person, forcing them to rely on the manipulator's version of the story.

On the other hand, silence can also be a method of withdrawing emotionally. This form of non-verbal communication happens when someone uses silence as a way to punish another person or signal disapproval without saying it outright. The famous "silent treatment" in relationships is a clear example of this. It's not just a quiet moment; it's a deliberate attempt to make the other person feel isolated, rejected, or unimportant. The person giving the silent treatment isn't just withholding words—they're using silence to communicate a message: "You've done something wrong, and now you'll feel the consequences."

The power of silence can also be used positively. It can be a tool for reflection, allowing both parties in a conversation time to think through their words and actions. In professional settings, silence can give a team space to process new information before reacting. In emotional situations, silence can provide both parties with a chance to calm down and think before escalating the conflict further. When used in the right way, silence becomes a tool for clarity, reflection, and understanding.

The next time you find yourself in a conversation where silence begins to stretch, pay attention to how it makes you feel. Are you uncomfortable? Are you second-guessing your words? Or are you giving space to reflect? Recognizing the power of silence in your own conversations can give you the ability to control the flow of communication and shift the dynamic in your favor.

Key Takeaways:

- **Silence creates emotional tension:** Silence can make people feel uneasy, forcing them to speak or act out of discomfort. Manipulators often use it to control the flow of conversations and push others into decisions.

- **Non-verbal cues can speak volumes:** Silence, combined with body language, can reveal more than words ever could. A moment of quiet can express authority, discomfort, or even disapproval, shifting the dynamics of any interaction without a word spoken.

- **Manipulators use silence to control situations. Whether withholding information or using silence to punish, manipulators know how** to force others into uncomfortable positions. Recognizing this tactic helps you protect yourself from being emotionally manipulated.

In this chapter, we've seen how silence can shape communication and how powerful it can be when used intentionally, whether for control or emotional influence. Now that you understand how silence can be a tool for manipulation, it's time to build your psychological defenses.

In Chapter 9, we'll explore how to recognize psychological triggers that leave you vulnerable and how you can develop emotional intelligence to protect yourself from being manipulated. Ready to strengthen your psychological immunity? Let's go.

Chapter 9:

Building Your Psychological Immunity

Your emotional vulnerabilities are not someone else's fault; they're your responsibility to manage. We like to think that the world is full of good people who wouldn't hurt us. We expect that if we're nice, others will reciprocate. The harsh reality is that we're constantly exposed to manipulative tactics, and if we're not careful, we'll fall victim to them time and time again. The only person who can truly protect you is you.

That's where psychological immunity comes in. Just as your body has an immune system to fight off illness, your mind needs its own defense mechanisms to handle the emotional and psychological attacks that come your way. Whether it's a manipulative coworker, an overly controlling partner, or a friend who pushes your boundaries, the ability to recognize and defend against these attacks starts with emotional intelligence (EI).

Emotional intelligence isn't just a buzzword; it's your armor in a world full of emotional traps. It's the ability to understand your own emotions and the emotions of others. More importantly, it's about using this awareness to guide your thinking and behavior, rather than letting your emotions control you. When you can identify psychological triggers—those emotional buttons manipulators push to get a reaction from you—you can stop them from getting the best of you. You no longer fall into their traps; you see them coming.

One of the first steps in building your psychological immunity is to recognize the emotional triggers you have. Do you react out of guilt when someone needs help, even if you don't have the time or energy? Do you feel anxious when others make you feel responsible for their emotions? Once you identify these patterns, you can start to manage them instead of letting them control you.

The next step is learning how to set healthy emotional boundaries. The more emotionally intelligent you become, the easier it is to protect your inner peace. You stop allowing others to manipulate your emotions and start taking control of your own. When you can guard your feelings, you become less susceptible to manipulation and more capable of making decisions that serve your best interests.

Recognizing Psychological Triggers That Make You Vulnerable

You have emotional triggers. Yes, you. Everyone does, even if they don't realize it. These triggers are the hidden buttons that manipulators press to get a response from you. The worst part? Most of the time, you don't even know you have them until someone taps into them.

They lie in the background of your emotional landscape, waiting for the right moment to be activated. The real secret is that your triggers can be used against you if you're unaware of them. That's why understanding them is so essential; the more you know about your own psychological vulnerabilities, the less power others have over you.

Imagine that someone you care about asks for your help, and even though you're exhausted or overwhelmed, you feel that tug, that guilt creeping in. You can't say no. The voice in your head starts convincing you that you're a bad person if you don't help. That's a trigger. The feeling of guilt can be such a powerful emotional trigger; it's like a psychological chain that locks you into doing something you don't want to do. Guilt isn't the only trigger that controls your decisions; there are plenty of others that manipulators use to control your emotions.

Let's dig into some of these psychological triggers. If you can recognize them in yourself, you can start to take control and protect yourself. You'll stop being a victim of others' emotional games and start living on your own terms.

- **The Guilt Trap**

This one is huge. You've probably experienced it more times than you realize. Someone asks you for a favor, and instead of saying "no," you feel a wave of guilt wash over you. You think, "If I don't help, they'll think I don't care," or "What kind of person would I be if I didn't lend a hand?" Guilt often comes from a deeply ingrained fear of being judged, rejected, or labeled as selfish. Manipulators know this. They know you'll feel guilty if you don't help, so they will use your guilt to their advantage.

CHAPTER 9: 87

They ask you for small favors, knowing that once you help, they'll ask for bigger ones. The more you give, the more they expect, and the more guilty you feel when you want to say no. The key here is realizing that guilt is not a valid reason to do something that doesn't serve your well-being. You are not obligated to put others before yourself constantly. You must learn to set boundaries and recognize that your value is not tied to how much you give or how many people you help.

- **The Fear of Missing Out (FOMO)**

You've probably felt this one a lot lately. It's that overwhelming sense of anxiety when everyone else seems to be having fun, experiencing life, or getting ahead, while you feel left behind. This fear is a powerful trigger because it taps into your insecurities. You're wired to want to belong to a group or to feel included. The more connected we are to others, the more secure we feel. Manipulators know that playing on your FOMO will drive you to act impulsively and make decisions based on fear rather than logic. Maybe someone invites you to an event, and you feel pressured to say yes, even though you're tired or it doesn't align with your values, simply because you don't want to miss out.

FOMO makes you feel like you're not enough, or like you're falling behind, so you feel you must act to keep up. Here's the truth—you are not defined by whether or not you're part of the crowd. You don't have to participate in everything. Recognize FOMO for what it is: an emotional ploy to get you to act out of fear rather than logic. When you feel the fear of missing out, ask yourself if you genuinely want to be part of it or if you're just afraid of being left out.

- **The Need for Approval**

How much do you crave approval from others? Be honest with yourself. If you're constantly seeking validation, it's a psychological trigger. From early childhood, we are conditioned to seek approval from our parents, teachers, friends, and even strangers. When someone's approval becomes a need, it's easy for others to use it against you. They know you'll go out of your way to get their stamp of approval, even if it means sacrificing your own desires or principles. People with this trigger will often find themselves saying "yes" to things they don't want to do, to make sure others like them.

Manipulators use this need for approval as a powerful tool. They might say things like, "I thought you'd want to help me, we're friends, aren't we?" Or they might give you positive reinforcement, then pull it back, making you chase after their approval. The real trap here is that you don't need anyone's approval to be worthy. You are valuable simply for being you. Start practicing self-acceptance and recognize when your actions are driven by a need for external validation, not your own genuine desire.

- **The Fear of Conflict**

This one can be subtle but incredibly powerful. If you avoid conflict at all costs, you're likely to find yourself in situations where you're walking on eggshells, trying to please everyone, and keeping the peace. Conflict feels uncomfortable, so to avoid it, you suppress your thoughts, feelings, or boundaries. The problem is, this leaves you vulnerable to manipulation. Manipulators will use your desire to avoid conflict to pressure you into agreeing with their agenda.

They know you'll give in to avoid an uncomfortable conversation. You might say yes to a request, even if it's unreasonable, to avoid confrontation. Recognize that avoiding conflict doesn't make it disappear. It just prolongs the tension and makes you feel powerless. Healthy conflict is essential for personal growth and for protecting your boundaries. When you feel the urge to avoid conflict, remind yourself that it's okay to speak your truth, even if it creates temporary discomfort. Your peace is worth fighting for.

- **The Desire to Be Needed**

We all want to feel important, valuable, and needed. Others often exploit this deep-seated desire. Manipulators know how to play on this—they'll make you feel indispensable, like you're the only one who can solve their problems or provide what they need. The feeling of being needed gives us a sense of purpose, so we give and give, hoping that others will appreciate us. The problem is, this often leads to self-sacrifice.

We end up saying yes to people, even when we know it's too much, all because we don't want to disappoint them. Recognize that your worth is not tied to how much you give or how indispensable you are to others. You are valuable simply for existing. Don't let others make you feel like you have to carry their emotional burdens. Learn to give without losing yourself in the process.

Recognizing these triggers is the first step in building your emotional intelligence. When you know what buttons can be pushed to make you react, you gain the power to protect yourself from being manipulated. The next step is learning how to take control of your emotions and strengthen your psychological immunity. This is your shield against manipulation—developing the ability to stay grounded, make decisions from a place of clarity, and stop being swayed by emotional pressure. It's time to take back control and make your decisions based on what you want, not what others manipulate you into doing.

How to Cultivate Emotional Intelligence to Stay Protected

Now that we've peeled back the layers of those psychological triggers and explored how manipulators use them to push our buttons, let's talk about how to build something even more substantial than your defenses. **Emotional intelligence (EI)** is your secret weapon. When you understand your emotions, control them, and know how to deal with other people's emotions, you can protect yourself from being manipulated. It's all about awareness, not just of your own feelings, but of the emotional landscape around you.

Here's the thing, though: emotional intelligence isn't just some abstract concept or a buzzword you hear at corporate seminars. It's a skill, just like any other skill; it can be developed. You can learn how to handle your emotions, read other people's emotional cues, and respond in ways that leave you in control, not at the mercy of your emotions or anyone else's. The more you grow your emotional intelligence, the better you'll become at navigating relationships, making decisions, and even protecting your boundaries.

Let's break it down, starting with the basics.

Self-awareness is the first building block of emotional intelligence. You can't protect yourself from emotional manipulation if you don't understand your own emotions. That might sound simple, but it's more difficult than it seems. You've probably felt like you're all over the place sometimes, frustrated one minute, excited the next, or maybe confused by a situation. Self-awareness is all about being able to step back and notice what you're feeling, when you're feeling it, and why.

Think about it like this: If you can identify what triggers your anger or fear, you can stop yourself from reacting in a way that leaves you vulnerable. Let's say someone says something rude to you, and you feel yourself getting worked up. If you don't stop and recognize that you're feeling triggered, you might lash out in anger or say something you regret. But if you stop for a moment, acknowledge that your anger is rising, and understand why, it becomes easier to control that emotion rather than letting it control you. Once you start practicing this, you'll find that your emotional reactions become more intentional and less about knee-jerk responses that leave you feeling out of control.

The next part of emotional intelligence is **self-regulation.** This is where you take your self-awareness and turn it into action. It's about managing your emotions, especially when they're trying to push you into a reaction. When someone triggers your guilt or makes you feel anxious, self-regulation is your ability to say, "Okay, I'm feeling guilty, but I'm going to take a step back and think about whether this feeling is valid." It's about not letting your emotions dictate your actions.

This skill isn't something that happens overnight. It takes practice, patience, and awareness. If you're in a situation where someone is pushing your emotional buttons, instead of reacting immediately, pause. Ask yourself what you're feeling, why you're feeling it, and what would be the best way to respond. Maybe it's taking a deep breath and saying "no" when you usually would have agreed. Perhaps it's recognizing that someone's guilt-tripping you and choosing to walk away, instead of falling into their emotional trap.

Empathy is another crucial piece of emotional intelligence. It's the ability to understand and share the feelings of others, but it's also a double-edged sword. When you can empathize with others, you know what they're going through, which is excellent when you want to build healthy relationships. Manipulators, though, will use your empathy to their advantage. They'll play on your desire to help, your willingness to be there for others, and make you feel like their emotions are your responsibility. Knowing how to empathize without falling into the trap of overextending yourself is critical.

Empathy helps you understand what's driving someone else's actions. Is the person pushing your buttons genuinely in need of support, or are they simply trying to manipulate you into doing something? Recognizing this is an essential part of protecting yourself. When you can empathize with others without getting caught up in their emotional manipulation, it allows you to respond with compassion while maintaining your boundaries. You might feel sympathy for someone, but that doesn't mean you have to give them everything they ask for. Empathy isn't about saying yes to everything. It's about being compassionate without losing yourself.

Now, let's talk about **social skills,** and I'm not talking about small talk or making friends at parties. I mean the ability to communicate effectively, build rapport, and manage relationships. A key component of emotional intelligence is being able to navigate social dynamics without being influenced by other people's emotional agendas. The better your social skills, the more easily you can read people and understand their intentions. If you can pick up on emotional cues—like body language, tone of voice, or facial expressions—you can recognize when someone's trying to manipulate you without saying it outright. This awareness gives you an edge. You won't be blindsided when someone tries to guilt-trip you, throw you off balance, or use fear to get what they want.

The beauty of emotional intelligence is that it empowers you to take control. You are no longer a passive participant in emotional exchanges, reacting to whatever is thrown your way. Instead, you actively manage your emotions, set boundaries, and communicate with clarity. It gives you the power to say 'no' when you need to, without feeling guilty or manipulated. It lets you handle difficult situations with confidence, and most importantly, it helps you stay emotionally protected from people who want to take advantage of your vulnerabilities.

In summary, emotional intelligence is your defense system. It protects you from being manipulated by giving you the tools to recognize emotional triggers, manage your responses, and communicate effectively. It helps you build stronger, healthier relationships by understanding both yourself and others. Developing emotional intelligence isn't an overnight process, but it's one of the best investments you can make for your mental and emotional well-being.

Key Takeaways:

- **Psychological triggers can be used against you:** Recognizing your emotional triggers is essential for protecting yourself from manipulation. By identifying patterns of guilt, FOMO, or the need for approval, you can stop others from exploiting your vulnerabilities.

- **Emotional intelligence helps you control your reactions:** Developing emotional intelligence lets you manage your emotions and make decisions from a place of clarity. It allows you to recognize manipulation early, set boundaries, and stay grounded in difficult situations.

- **Protecting yourself requires practice and self-awareness:** Building psychological immunity takes time. By cultivating emotional intelligence and learning to recognize triggers, you can safeguard your mental well-being and ensure that others don't manipulate your emotions or push you into decisions you don't want.

This chapter shows how emotional intelligence and self-awareness are the building blocks of your psychological defense system. Once you recognize your emotional triggers, you gain control over your reactions and interactions.

Moving forward, we'll explore another way to enhance your emotional resilience by building a stronger mindset. In the next chapter, we'll discuss how having multiple choices can reduce manipulative control. By empowering yourself with options, you'll discover a newfound sense of freedom and confidence.

Chapter 10:

The Power of Choice: Building a Stronger Mind

Have you ever been in a situation where you felt completely cornered? Maybe it was in a conversation, a decision-making moment, or even a relationship where it seemed like there was only one way out. You felt as though your options were limited, and the pressure of choosing the "right" one was overwhelming. What if I told you that feeling is often the result of having fewer choices than you actually have? Manipulators know this all too well. They thrive when they limit your options, leaving you with only one course of action to take—theirs.

So, how do you regain control when it feels like your options are being taken away? How do you build a mindset that empowers you to feel free, no matter the situation? The answer lies in choice. Having multiple options is one of the most effective ways to reduce manipulative control. When you recognize that you have the power to make decisions, you regain the freedom to choose what aligns with your values, needs, and desires.

How often do you find yourself accepting what someone else offers without exploring the other alternatives? Why do we tend to give in when we're presented with only one option, even when deep down, we know there are others? What would happen if we trained ourselves to recognize all the choices available to us, even when they're hidden behind a veil of pressure or guilt?

In this chapter, we'll explore how to cultivate a mindset of freedom through the power of choice. We'll talk about how to recognize when your choices are being limited and how to expand your options, even in the most constrained situations. The more options you see, the more power you have. The more power you have, the less control others can exert over your decisions. It's time to shift from a mindset of scarcity to one of abundance.

Why Having Multiple Options Reduces Manipulative Control

Let's say you're standing in front of a door with two signs: one says "Enter" and the other says "Stay Out." These are the only two choices you're given. You can either go through the door or you can walk away. Now, the only thing standing between you and a decision is the pressure of choosing the "right" option. How does it feel? It feels a bit intense, doesn't it? The pressure of selecting the "correct" one, knowing there's no middle ground. That's the feeling of having limited options—like you're stuck in a binary situation. The choices seem absolute and rigid, almost like you have no control over what happens next.

Now, imagine the same scenario, but this time, you're standing in front of five doors—each one has a sign with a different option. Some doors still say "Enter" while others say "Stay Out", but now, you also have doors labeled "Pause and Think", "Explore More Options", and "Consider the Consequences". All of a sudden, the decision doesn't feel so overwhelming. You have choices. You have freedom. Even if the stakes are high, you now feel empowered to weigh your options. Instead of feeling forced into a "right or wrong" decision, you can navigate through the choices in a way that feels more natural and informed.

This is the power of having multiple options. When you can see several ways forward, the pressure of making a choice doesn't feel so intense. You aren't stuck in a corner. You can breathe and think. Having more choices creates freedom. Freedom to decide, freedom to think clearly, and freedom to make a choice that aligns with your needs and desires.

At its core, having multiple options means you aren't trapped in a binary thinking mindset, where only one choice seems possible. In these situations, you typically feel stuck, as if there's only one clear course of action, often dictated by someone else. Instead, when you have more options, your mind begins to open. You stop seeing your decisions as limited, and instead, you start thinking in terms of possibilities. It's like expanding your vision—suddenly, there's more space to move, more routes to consider, and more angles to look at. The world feels more flexible when you can see multiple possibilities. It doesn't feel like a rigid, one-way street where someone else is pulling the strings.

The true power of having multiple options is in the ability to choose. Without it, you can easily fall victim to external influences. If someone only offers you one option and pressures you into taking it, it becomes much harder to say "no." Your mind becomes focused solely on that one choice, making it difficult to consider alternatives or evaluate whether this option truly serves you. With multiple choices, you don't feel as pressured or as vulnerable. When the options are available, you can step back, take a moment, and actively choose what feels right. You're in control.

The next aspect of having multiple options is mental flexibility. When you are faced with only one choice, the ability to adapt your thinking or adjust your decision-making process is severely limited. You can only go one way, and that's the end of it. But when you have multiple options, you can pivot. You can adjust your decision based on new information, new perspectives, or a change in circumstances. Mental flexibility is the ability to look at a situation and assess it from various angles. The more options you have, the more adaptable you can be. You're no longer confined to a narrow path; you're free to make decisions based on what's best for you in the moment.

Let's think about decision-making for a moment. Have you ever had a situation where you had to make an important decision quickly, but you only had one option on the table? If you've been there, you know how overwhelming that can feel. There's no room for error, and there is no chance to reconsider. With just one choice, your mind becomes laser-focused on it, pushing aside other considerations. Now think about a time when you had more than one option to choose from. Suddenly, it doesn't feel as stressful. You can weigh the pros and cons, think through the risks, and then confidently make your decision.

This flexibility in decision-making reduces stress and increases confidence. It gives you a sense of control that's hard to achieve when you feel cornered. When you're able to explore different options, your mind becomes more resourceful. You start asking better questions, considering what you really need, and ultimately making better decisions.

There's also the emotional benefit of having multiple options. When you feel like you have control over your choices, you're much more likely to feel empowered and secure. Think about it. Have you ever felt a little bit overwhelmed by a situation where it seemed like you had no choice? It's like being forced into a corner where you feel stuck with whatever comes your way. Now imagine that same situation, but this time you see multiple ways forward. You can breathe easier, knowing that if one path doesn't work, there's another option you can try. The emotional weight of the decision lessens when there's more flexibility in your choices.

Having multiple options also allows you to create more opportunities. Sometimes, when we limit ourselves to only one way of doing things, we close off the possibility of something better. With more choices, you open up the door to new experiences, growth, and potential. You can say, "If this doesn't work, I'll try this," or "If I don't like this path, I can take another." You're no longer tied to just one outcome. There's freedom in knowing that failure or mistakes won't trap you; they'll simply open the door to a new possibility.

In summary, having multiple options allows you to take control of your decisions, reduce stress, and make empowered choices. The more options you have, the more flexibility you have in making decisions that serve your best interests, instead of feeling pushed into a decision that doesn't align with you.

How to Cultivate a Mindset of Freedom and Empowerment

In the movie The Lion King, Simba's journey is a perfect example of how cultivating a mindset of freedom and empowerment can completely change the course of one's life. Think about it: Simba starts off as a carefree cub, full of potential, but he allows his fears and guilt to control his life. He runs away from his responsibilities, pushing aside his identity and the legacy of his father. It's only when he faces his past and realizes his true strength that he can finally step into his role as king.

This shift in mindset is the key to personal empowerment. It recognizes that true freedom isn't just about what's happening around you but what's happening inside of you.

Simba's story is more than just a tale of adventure and courage. It's a metaphor for how we often allow fear, guilt, and self-doubt to hold us back from achieving our true potential. We get stuck in our own emotional traps, not realizing that the power to change is within us. Just like Simba, you can choose to confront your fears, let go of past mistakes, and step into the person you were always meant to be. The mindset that Simba adopts, a mentality of freedom and empowerment, isn't something that happens by accident. It's something you have to work on every day actively.

Freedom isn't just about external circumstances. It's easy to think that freedom means doing whatever you want, whenever you want. However, absolute freedom begins within. It starts with taking ownership of your choices. Simba wasn't free when he was running away from his responsibilities. He wasn't free when he was avoiding the throne. He was free only when he accepted his true self and embraced his responsibility. Freedom comes from realizing that you have the power to make your own decisions and shape your own future. This realization is empowering; it takes away the sense of helplessness and replaces it with confidence and purpose.

Let's think about how we often limit ourselves. We may feel stuck in jobs we don't like, in relationships that drain us, or in situations that feel out of our control. The common thread in these situations is a feeling of having no options. We assume we're trapped because we believe that our only choice is to continue the path we're on. However, the truth is that there are always options; sometimes, we just need to open our minds to them. Simba doesn't realize he has a choice until he is confronted with the truth about himself. We all have choices, even when it feels like we're backed into a corner.

One of the most essential things Simba learns on his journey is that freedom comes from taking responsibility for your actions. When he returns to the Pride Lands and faces his uncle Scar, Simba's true strength is revealed not in his physical power, but in his willingness to take ownership of his past mistakes. He doesn't let the guilt of Mufasa's death weigh him down anymore. He chooses to accept what happened and move forward. The power of this shift is incredible. He frees himself from his past and steps into his true potential. Similarly, in our own lives, when we refuse to take responsibility for our actions, we stay stuck in the past. We keep making excuses, blaming others, or letting guilt prevent us from moving forward. The moment you take responsibility for your life is the moment you start to regain control.

Another key lesson from Simba's journey is embracing self-empowerment. Throughout the movie, Simba learns that his power isn't about defeating others or proving something to the world; it's about recognizing the strength within himself. When you're constantly looking for external validation, you give up your personal power. You depend on others to tell you who you are and what you should do. Simba's transformation occurs when he accepts who he truly is, the king. Self-empowerment comes from within. It's about knowing your worth, trusting your abilities, and not waiting for permission from anyone else. You don't need anyone else to validate your worth. You are powerful simply because you are you.

Empowerment also requires surrounding yourself with people who support your growth. Simba's friends, Timon and Pumbaa, are there for him through thick and thin. They encourage him to embrace who he is, to stop running away from his past, and to face the challenges ahead. It's essential to have people who uplift you and remind you of your potential. When you surround yourself with the right people, those who believe in you, you start believing in yourself. The people you choose to have in your life can either build you up or tear you down. If you find yourself around people who don't support your growth or make you feel small, it's time to reevaluate who you allow in your circle.

One of the most powerful takeaways from Simba's story is that empowerment is a choice. Just like Simba, you have the power to decide whether to embrace your potential or keep running away. You have the freedom to determine if you will continue letting fear or guilt control your life, or whether you'll take control of your narrative. The truth is, no one can empower you except yourself. Empowerment starts with the decision to step into your power, to make decisions that align with your actual values, and to stop letting external circumstances dictate your happiness or success.

To wrap it all up, cultivating a mindset of freedom and empowerment is about understanding that you are not a victim of your circumstances. You are not defined by your past mistakes or the limitations others put on you. When you embrace your power, take responsibility, and surround yourself with the right people, you start to create a life that genuinely reflects who you are. You begin to make choices that align with your values, desires, and vision for the future. Just like Simba, you are the king or queen of your life, and it's time to embrace that power fully.

Key Takeaways:

- **Having multiple options gives you control:** When you have choices, you reduce the influence others can have on your decisions. More options mean more freedom to act according to your true desires, rather than being pushed into a corner.

- **Freedom is rooted in decision-making:** Empowerment comes from the ability to make decisions that align with your values. Cultivating a mindset of freedom involves recognizing your right to choose your path, no matter the pressures around you.

- **Choices create mental flexibility and resilience:** A mindset of freedom grows stronger when you recognize that you are not trapped by one way of thinking. The more options you see, the more adaptable and confident you become in navigating life's challenges.

This chapter highlighted how the freedom to choose empowers you and reduces the control others can have over your decisions. The more choices you see, the more in charge you are. Now that you understand the power of choice, let's move on to the next step.

Moving on, we'll explore how to identify manipulative tactics and decode the moves people use to push your buttons. By recognizing these tactics, you'll be better equipped to protect yourself from those who seek to control your choices.

Chapter 11:

Decoding Their Moves: Identifying Manipulative Tactics

I still laugh when I think about the time I tried to convince my little brother to help me with a chore. I had a massive pile of laundry to fold, and I was desperate for some help. So, I pulled out all the stops and said, "You know, if you help me out, I'll let you pick the movie tonight." It sounded like a fair trade, right? He agreed. Later, I found out he was planning to play video games the entire night, altogether avoiding the "deal" we'd made. I was frustrated but also laughing at how I had just made a classic mistake. I thought my offer would be enough to manipulate him into doing what I wanted, but he saw right through it.

That day, I learned that people can sometimes use tactics, subtle or direct, to get what they want from you. It happens more than we realize. Whether it's a simple favor or a big decision, manipulators understand that influencing emotions can be just as powerful as any direct argument or logical reasoning. They know how to use tactics that make you feel like you don't have a choice, making you comply without even realizing it.

What I didn't see in the moment was that I was setting myself up for manipulation. I was trying to use guilt (because my brother had no reason not to help me) and the promise of a reward to get him to do something. It was an innocent attempt to get help, but it's a prime example of how even subtle attempts to influence someone can be manipulative.

In this chapter, we'll explore the 10 most common manipulative tactics people use to control, influence, or coerce others. From guilt-tripping to emotional blackmail, manipulators use these methods to get you to do what they want, often without you even realizing it. Learning how to recognize these tactics can help you stay in control of your choices and protect your peace.

The 10 Most Common Manipulative Tactics and How to Recognize Them

Manipulation isn't always loud or obvious. Sometimes, it's sneaky and quiet, a tactic that sneaks into a conversation or a relationship without you even realizing it. Manipulative tactics often play on your emotions, making you feel guilty, confused, or responsible for someone else's needs. Here are the 10 most common manipulative tactics and how to spot them before they have a chance to control you.

- **Guilt-Tripping:**

One of the oldest tricks in the book is guilt-tripping. Manipulators know that guilt is a powerful emotion. They'll use it to make you feel responsible for their feelings or actions. For example, someone might say, "I thought you cared about me, but I guess I was wrong," to make you feel bad and get you to do something for them. Recognizing guilt-tripping is simple: if someone tries to make you feel guilty for something that's not your responsibility, they're using this tactic. Don't let their emotional weight dictate your actions. You don't have to take on their emotions.

- **Emotional Blackmail:**

This tactic is a step further than guilt-tripping. With emotional blackmail, a person uses your emotions to threaten or pressure you into doing what they want. They might say something like, "If you don't help me with this, I don't know how I'll survive." They're essentially trying to make you feel like their well-being is on the line if you don't comply. Recognizing emotional blackmail can be tough, but if someone's trying to make you feel responsible for their happiness or survival, it's time to step back. You are not responsible for their emotional state.

- **Gaslighting:**

Gaslighting is one of the most insidious manipulative tactics. It's a form of psychological manipulation where the manipulator makes you doubt your own perception of reality. They might deny things you clearly saw or heard, leaving you questioning your sanity. For example, if someone tells you, "That never happened," even though you know it did, they're gaslighting you. The trick here is to trust your instincts. If someone consistently makes you feel confused or unsure of your reality, recognize it as gaslighting. You know what you experienced—don't let anyone make you second-guess yourself.

- **Playing the Victim:**

When someone is constantly playing the victim, it's a manipulative tactic. They'll make themselves seem helpless, like they have no control over their situation, and then guilt you into helping them. You might hear something like, "I always get the short end of the stick. Why does this always happen to me?" The goal here is to make you feel sorry for them and step in to "rescue" them. Recognize when someone is exaggerating their hardships to manipulate your feelings. You don't owe anyone your help just because they make you feel sorry for them.

- **Love Bombing:**

At the start of a relationship, manipulators will often overwhelm you with affection, compliments, and promises. This is known as love bombing. They'll shower you with love and attention to get you hooked, only to pull back later and leave you craving more. The aim is to make you feel special and wanted, only to use that emotional dependence to control you later. If someone is suddenly over-the-top affectionate or constantly telling you how perfect you are, it might be a sign of love bombing. Healthy relationships build over time—not through sudden bursts of intense affection.

- **Silent Treatment:**

The silent treatment is a form of manipulation where someone refuses to communicate with you in order to punish you or get their way. They'll act like they're upset with you, leaving you confused and anxious, wondering what you did wrong. The goal is to get you to chase after them for validation or to apologize, even when you're not sure what you've done. If someone is refusing to talk to you, ask yourself whether they're using silence to control you. Healthy communication is key—no one should have the power to control your emotions through silence.

- **Flattery for Control:**

Flattery is usually seen as a harmless compliment, but manipulators use excessive flattery to lower your guard and make you more compliant. They'll tell you things like, "You're so much smarter than everyone else. I just knew you'd be the one to help me," to make you feel special and trusted. Then, they'll ask you for favors or to do something for them. Recognize when compliments are given with the expectation of something in return. Genuine compliments come without hidden agendas. Trust actions, not just words.

- **Overloading You with Information:**

Sometimes, manipulators will overwhelm you with excessive details to confuse you and cloud your judgment. This tactic, often known as information overload, makes it difficult to process everything, leaving you uncertain about what's actually essential. If someone constantly bombards you with irrelevant information, they may be trying to distract you from the real issue or decision. Cut through the noise by asking clear, direct questions to get to the heart of the matter. Don't let someone bury you in unnecessary details.

- **Shifting Blame:**

When something goes wrong, manipulators will shift the blame to you, making you feel like it's your fault, even if it isn't. They'll say things like, "This wouldn't have happened if you had just done X," or "You made me react this way." They deflect responsibility, making you feel responsible for their actions or feelings. Recognizing blame-shifting is easy; if someone constantly points fingers and avoids taking responsibility for their mistakes, they're manipulating you. Hold others accountable for their actions.

- **Playing on Your Fears:**

One of the most effective tactics is using fear to get you to act in a certain way. They might say things like, "What if something happens to you and you don't act now?" or "If you don't do this, there could be consequences." This is manipulating your fear to pressure you into making a decision you wouldn't usually make. When you feel fear, step back and ask yourself whether this fear is being used to control you. Fear should never be the driver of your decisions.

These 10 manipulative tactics are often used to push your emotional buttons and gain control over your decisions. The more you recognize them, the less power they have over you.

How to Analyze Situations to Detect Hidden Manipulations

Have you ever walked out of a conversation feeling uneasy, but couldn't quite put your finger on why? Maybe someone said all the right things, but something about the situation didn't sit right with you. You couldn't figure out whether you were overthinking things or if there was something more to it. This happens when manipulation is at play—it's often subtle, and the manipulator's goal is to make you feel like you're the one who's being unreasonable. The good news is that with a bit of practice, you can learn how to spot these hidden manipulations and take back control of your decisions.

When you're faced with a situation, it's essential to stop for a moment and pause before reacting. This gives you the space to observe the situation more objectively, without rushing into a decision you might later regret. Manipulation thrives on impulse reactions—the more you can control your knee-jerk responses, the easier it becomes to spot when something is off. Take a moment to ask yourself: "Is this really my decision, or is someone else trying to influence me without me realizing it?" This simple question can give you a lot of insight into what's going on.

One of the first steps in analyzing a situation for hidden manipulation is to pay attention to the emotions at play. Manipulators love to play on your feelings, pushing your buttons in ways that make you feel guilty, fearful, or responsible for their happiness. If you're suddenly feeling overwhelmed or pressured, it's a sign that something might be going on beneath the surface. Ask yourself: why do I feel this way? If the answer is because someone is making you feel responsible for their emotions or trying to guilt you into doing something, chances are you're being manipulated. Emotional manipulation is about making you feel something, often against your will.

Another way to detect hidden manipulation is to pay attention to the timing of the situation. Manipulators often create a sense of urgency to get you to act without thinking. If someone is trying to rush you into making a decision or pushing you into a corner, it's essential to slow down. A classic manipulative tactic is making you feel like there's a limited window of opportunity, forcing you to decide quickly. When that happens, take a step back. Ask yourself, is this truly urgent, or am I being rushed to make a choice too fast? When you have time to think and assess, you'll be able to make a more informed decision, free from the pressure they're trying to put on you.

Body language is another key indicator of manipulation. People often send subtle messages with their bodies that they don't even realize. When someone is trying to manipulate you, they may use closed-off body language, such as crossing their arms or avoiding eye contact. These are signs that they're trying to shield themselves from vulnerability or exert control over the situation. On the other hand, manipulative people may also use overly open body language—like leaning in too close or making too much eye contact—to create a sense of intimacy or trust while still controlling the interaction. Pay attention to how someone's body language shifts as the conversation goes on. If their words say one thing but their body is saying another, that's a red flag.

Another sign of manipulation is when someone keeps changing the topic or avoiding direct answers. This tactic is used to distract you from the issue at hand or deflect attention away from their true intentions. If someone constantly brings up unrelated points or gives vague, evasive answers when you ask direct questions, they're likely trying to control the flow of the conversation to make you feel confused or unsure. It's essential to stay focused and keep bringing the conversation back to the key points that matter to you. When you notice these shifts, it's a sign that the other person is trying to steer you away from making clear decisions or seeing the truth.

Observe the consistency between words and actions. Manipulators often use charming words to pull you in, making promises they may never keep. If someone says one thing but their actions tell a different story, that's a huge red flag. For example, they might say, "I care about you," but their actions consistently show a lack of respect for your boundaries or feelings. In these situations, it's crucial to trust your observations over words. Actions speak louder than words, and when someone's behavior doesn't align with their promises, manipulation is likely at play. If someone is being overly sweet or overly apologetic to cover up bad actions, take note of the inconsistencies.

Another critical aspect of analyzing manipulation is the use of guilt or sympathy. Manipulators will often try to make you feel bad for them to get what they want. They'll make you feel like you're the one who is wrong for setting boundaries, or they'll try to get you to feel sorry for them, even when they don't deserve it. For instance, if someone says, "You're the only one who hasn't helped me out. Don't you care?" This is a classic guilt-tripping tactic. They'll try to make you feel selfish or inconsiderate, making you feel like you owe them. Please recognize that this is an attempt to control your emotions and get you to act on their behalf.

Finally, listen to your gut. If something feels off, it probably is. Your instincts are often the first line of defense against manipulation. When you sense that something isn't right, trust that feeling and dig deeper into the situation. Your intuition can often pick up on things your conscious mind hasn't fully processed yet. If you feel pressured, uncomfortable, or like your boundaries are being crossed, don't ignore it. Take the time to step back, reassess, and choose what's best for you.

Key Takeaways:

- **Recognizing manipulative tactics is crucial for self-defense:** Manipulators use various tactics like guilt-tripping, gaslighting, and emotional blackmail to control you. Identifying these behaviors early helps you protect your boundaries and make empowered decisions.

- **Understanding emotional manipulation improves decision-making:** When you're aware of how others try to influence your emotions, you can step back and assess situations more clearly. Recognizing manipulative tactics ensures that your choices are based on your needs, not emotional pressure.

- **Trust your instincts when detecting manipulation:** Your gut feelings often reveal when something's off. When you sense discomfort or confusion in a situation, it's a sign to dig deeper, analyze the behavior, and protect your emotional well-being.

In this chapter, we've learned how to recognize the most common manipulative tactics that people use to control or influence others. By becoming aware of these behaviors, you empower yourself to make better decisions.

With this knowledge, you are ready to take the next step: walking away. Refusing to engage with manipulators and choosing to protect your peace is one of the most powerful ways to regain control. Are you ready to discover how disengaging can shift the power in your favor? Let's move forward.

Chapter 12:

Walking Away Is the Most Powerful Form of Control

It might sound counterintuitive at first, but sometimes the most powerful thing you can do in a situation is simply walk away. When we're faced with a manipulator trying to control our emotions, decisions, or actions, the instinctive reaction is often to push back, argue, or prove a point. However, the most effective way to regain control is by refusing to engage. Silence is stronger than words. By choosing not to react, you maintain your peace and make a statement that you cannot be easily manipulated.

I remember a time when I was involved in a heated discussion with a friend who was constantly pushing my buttons, trying to guilt me into doing something I didn't want to do. The more I tried to explain myself, the more they turned the conversation around to make me feel responsible for their frustration. The longer we argued, the more I realized I wasn't getting through. Then, I made a choice. I stopped responding, stood up, and walked away. At first, it felt like I was losing, like I wasn't standing my ground. However, the real victory came in the silence that followed. They were left to face their emotions, and I protected my peace.

Walking away doesn't mean surrendering or avoiding conflict. It means taking control of your emotional state, recognizing that you don't have to engage with anything that drains or manipulates you. It's a powerful decision to disengage, to protect your inner peace from external chaos. In this chapter, we'll explore how refusing to engage with manipulators not only protects your mental and emotional well-being but also shifts the power dynamic in your favor. It's time to learn how to walk away with confidence and regain control over your life.

How Refusing to Engage with Manipulators Puts You in Control

When you're dealing with manipulators, it's easy to fall into the trap of constantly reacting to their tactics. You might feel the need to explain yourself, defend your position, or even appease them. However, the most powerful thing you can do is walk away. Refusing to engage doesn't mean giving up; it means taking control of the situation and protecting your peace.

Here's how walking away puts you in charge:

- **You stop the manipulation cycle:**

Manipulators thrive on the emotional reactions they get from you. They know how to push your buttons to make you react, whether it's through guilt, anger, or fear. When you refuse to engage, you break that cycle. By stepping away or simply remaining silent, you remove the emotional fuel they need to continue manipulating you. They no longer have the power to control your emotions. You become the one calling the shots on how you react.

- **It shows you value yourself:**

Walking away is a bold act of self-respect. It's saying, "I know my worth, and I will not allow myself to be emotionally drained by you." Manipulators often target people they perceive as vulnerable or willing to give in. By refusing to engage, you show that you will not let someone else's behavior dictate your emotional state. Setting boundaries in this way demonstrates that you value your peace and well-being more than the manipulator's agenda.

- **You take control of the situation's pace:**

Manipulators often want to control the timing and outcome of an interaction. They'll push you into a corner, expecting you to react immediately or give in to their demands. When you refuse to engage, you take control of the situation's pace. You decide when or if you'll respond. This gives you time to think, process, and make decisions that are in your best interest, rather than being rushed into a response that you'll regret later.

- **It forces the manipulator to face their own behavior:**

When you walk away or refuse to engage, you're forcing the manipulator to confront their own behavior. Manipulators thrive on getting away with their tactics, often leaving you questioning yourself. When you disengage, it disrupts their ability to use their tactics to manipulate the situation. They are left to deal with the consequences of their own actions, rather than you reacting to their emotional cues.

- **You maintain your emotional peace:**

Engaging with manipulators often leads to frustration, anger, or feelings of helplessness. Manipulators know how to use these emotions against you, leaving you mentally and emotionally drained. When you refuse to engage, you're preserving your emotional well-being. Instead of getting caught up in a battle, you maintain a sense of calm and clarity, which ultimately allows you to make decisions that align with your actual values and not the manipulator's agenda.

- **You regain control over your power and energy:**

Manipulators will often use emotional energy as a tool to wear you down. Whether it's through constant demands, guilt trips, or playing on your fears, they feed off the energy you give them. By walking away, you reclaim your personal energy. You stop giving it to someone who wants to use it to control you, and you preserve it for things and people that matter. This return of energy is a form of self-care and empowerment.

- **You set a powerful precedent for future interactions:**

When you practice walking away, you set a firm boundary that others will begin to respect. If manipulators see that you will not tolerate their behavior and refuse to engage, they will likely back off. Over time, you'll find that people will learn how to approach you with more respect. You become known for protecting your peace, which can be a powerful deterrent for anyone thinking of manipulating you in the future.

- **You stop feeling responsible for their emotions:**

Manipulators often try to make you feel responsible for their emotional states. They might say things like, "You're the only one who can help me" or "Why are you doing this to me?" The truth is, you are not responsible for anyone's emotions except your own. When you refuse to engage, you're telling them that you won't take on their emotional baggage. You stop being manipulated by their guilt trips, and you no longer feel the weight of their emotions pressing down on you.

- **You empower yourself to walk away from toxic situations:**

Refusing to engage is a sign of strength. It allows you to walk away from toxic situations, whether it's a conversation, a relationship, or a work environment. Choosing to disengage is your way of saying, "I will not be a part of this." Walking away doesn't mean you're avoiding the situation; it means you're choosing peace over chaos, respect over manipulation, and empowerment over control. By doing so, you create a safe space for yourself, where you can thrive without being dragged into toxic dynamics.

- **It creates space for better communication:**

When you walk away from a manipulative conversation or situation, it allows for more transparent communication later on. Manipulation thrives in confusion and emotional pressure. By refusing to engage, you give both yourself and the manipulator the time and space needed to process emotions. This opens the door for healthier, more constructive conversations down the line, where both parties can communicate more openly and honestly.

In summary, walking away from a manipulative situation is one of the most powerful tools you have. It puts you in control by protecting your peace, maintaining your energy, and setting boundaries. The more you practice disengaging, the stronger and more empowered you'll feel.

CHAPTER 12:

The Strength in Disengagement and Protecting Your Peace

It can be tough to walk away from a conversation or situation, especially when emotions are running high. We often feel like we have to stick it out, explain ourselves, or defend our position. The idea of simply disengaging might feel like we're giving up or admitting defeat. However, in reality, the power of disengagement lies in its ability to protect your emotional and mental peace. Choosing to step away, not to engage, is one of the strongest moves you can make to ensure that you stay in control and maintain your well-being.

When we engage in situations that are emotionally charged or manipulative, we can easily find ourselves caught up in a whirlwind of stress, frustration, and confusion. Manipulators know how to trigger our emotions and push our buttons. They feed off our reactions, using them to further their own agendas. If you've ever found yourself in a conversation where you feel drained or manipulated, you know how hard it can be to walk away. You might feel guilty, like you're abandoning the situation or the person, or like you're avoiding the conflict. The reality, though, is that walking away is not avoidance. It's a conscious decision to protect your peace, stop the cycle of emotional manipulation, and give yourself the space to think clearly.

Disengagement allows you to break free from the emotional control manipulators try to gain over you. Think of it as pressing pause when everything around you feels like it's spiraling out of control. It creates distance between you and the situation, allowing you to regain perspective. When you disengage, you no longer react impulsively. You take back your power and refuse to let someone else dictate how you feel. This distance gives you the chance to breathe, reflect, and decide how you want to proceed, rather than reacting out of emotional pressure.

In moments where you feel manipulated or pressured into doing something, walking away is your way of taking back control. Manipulators often use guilt, fear, or confusion to get you to act in a way that benefits them. If you give in, you may end up feeling like you lost yourself in the process. Disengagement helps you maintain your integrity, keeping you from doing things you might regret later. It allows you to step outside of the emotional chaos and assess the situation from a place of calm. By disengaging, you show that you're not going to let someone else's tactics dictate your actions. You protect your sense of self, refusing to be manipulated.

Another key benefit of disengagement is that it sends a clear message to manipulators. People who try to manipulate others often rely on emotional pressure to get their way. When you disengage, you break their pattern. They are left with no audience for their tactics. Manipulators thrive on getting a reaction, so when you refuse to engage, they lose their power. It's like pulling the rug out from under them—without your emotional involvement, their manipulative behavior has no foundation to stand on. This doesn't mean you have to be rude or dismissive. Simply walking away with a calm, composed attitude makes it clear that you will no longer tolerate being controlled.

Disengagement also allows you to maintain emotional balance. When you constantly engage in arguments or stressful situations, it's easy to feel emotionally drained. Our emotional energy is limited, and when we're caught up in toxic dynamics, we're often left feeling exhausted and depleted. Walking away from these situations allows you to conserve your energy, keeping you focused on what really matters. Instead of getting caught up in a hostile back-and-forth, you can protect your emotional health by stepping away. It's a form of self-care. You're protecting your peace and making sure you have the energy to deal with situations that align with your goals and values.

Furthermore, disengagement teaches you to set healthy boundaries. Healthy boundaries are essential for protecting your peace and maintaining control over your life. If you constantly engage with emotionally manipulative people, you'll find yourself in a constant battle to keep your sense of self. Walking away is a form of boundary-setting. It says, "I will not tolerate this behavior," and "I choose my own emotional state." It's an act of self-respect and self-preservation. By disengaging, you're saying that your peace is non-negotiable. No one has the right to invade that peace with manipulative behavior.

In many cases, manipulators will try to guilt you into engaging by making you feel like you're being rude or dismissive. They may try to make you feel like walking away is a sign of weakness or cowardice. This is where your inner strength comes into play. Disengagement requires confidence. It requires the understanding that you don't have to engage with people or situations that are draining or toxic. You don't have to justify your decision to walk away, either. Your peace is more important than anyone else's attempt to control you.

Lastly, disengagement allows for mental clarity. Sometimes, in the heat of the moment, emotions cloud our judgment. When you're stuck in a manipulative situation, your thoughts can become jumbled and unclear. Walking away gives you the space you need to step back, reflect, and see things from a more objective perspective. You'll be able to analyze the situation more clearly, free from the emotional pressure that manipulators try to create. With this clarity, you can make better decisions, ones that align with your values and protect your peace.

In summary, disengagement is one of the most powerful ways to protect your peace and regain control over your emotions. It allows you to avoid being manipulated, conserve your emotional energy, and set healthy boundaries. Choosing to walk away is an act of strength, not weakness. It sends a clear message that you are in control of your emotional state and will not allow anyone to manipulate you into decisions that aren't in your best interest.

Key Takeaways:

- **Disengagement is a powerful tool for regaining control:** Walking away from manipulative situations allows you to regain control over your emotions and decisions. It prevents you from being swayed by others' emotional tactics or pressure.

- **Refusing to engage protects your peace:** Disengaging from manipulators helps you preserve your mental and emotional well-being. It creates space for clarity, emotional balance, and personal boundaries, allowing you to make decisions based on what aligns with your values.

- **Walking away sends a clear message:** When you disengage, you show that you will not tolerate manipulative behavior. It forces manipulators to face the consequences of their actions while leaving you in control of the situation and your own peace.

In this final chapter, we've learned how walking away is one of the most powerful ways to protect your peace and maintain control over your life. Disengagement isn't a sign of weakness; it's a tool for self-empowerment.

Choosing to step back from a manipulative situation can create space for clarity, preserve your emotional energy, and set firm boundaries for your well-being. The strength in disengagement lies in your ability to control the situation and protect your peace without sacrificing your values or integrity. This gives you the power to make decisions with a clear mind, free from emotional pressure.

Conclusion

Wow. We've covered a lot of ground in this book!

Together, we've explored how manipulation works, how to spot it, and most importantly, how to take control and protect your mental and emotional peace. It's not always easy to recognize when someone is trying to manipulate you. Often, manipulation comes in the form of guilt, fear, emotional pressure, or even subtle body language. These are tactics we all encounter in life, sometimes without even realizing it. However, the most important thing you've learned from this book is that you have the power to recognize, respond, and ultimately protect yourself.

In Chapter 1, we started by discussing the hidden forces of influence—the psychological triggers that shape our decisions and actions without us even being aware of them. Understanding these invisible hands that guide our choices was just the beginning. Once you become aware of how cognitive biases, social pressures, and emotional appeals affect your decision-making, you can start to make more intentional, empowered choices. It's about realizing that you are not a passive participant in the decisions you make.

By recognizing these hidden forces, you take the first step toward taking control.

From there, we dove into the anatomy of a lie in Chapter 2. Lies are everywhere. Whether they are told to protect someone's ego, cover up mistakes, or manipulate you into doing something, lies are a tool often used to get what one wants. Understanding the cognitive and emotional structures behind lies helps you decode them, even when the liar is incredibly convincing. It's easy to fall into the trap of believing something because it aligns with what we want to hear. Being able to spot a lie—not just the words, but the body language, the hesitation, the inconsistencies—is a skill that can save you from a lot of unnecessary trouble.

In Chapter 3, we continued unraveling the masks people wear. It's human nature to hide behind a persona or mask to protect ourselves from vulnerability or judgment. Understanding why people wear these masks, and why we do, too, can help you navigate social interactions more effectively. When you see someone's mask, you can start to look beyond it and understand their true motivations. This is key to building better, more authentic relationships and ensuring you're not misled by someone's appearance or words alone.

In Chapter 4, we explored how the body never lies. Your body is constantly giving you clues about what's really going on underneath the surface. Whether it's the subtle twitch of an eye, the way someone shifts their posture, or the tightness in their voice, these signals speak volumes. People can lie with their words, but their body tells the real story. Learning to read these signals puts you in a position of power—you'll no longer be left in the dark about someone's true intentions.

Eyes are often referred to as the windows to the soul, and in Chapter 5, we learned just how true that is. What different eye movements reveal about someone's truth is fascinating. Eye contact (or lack of it) can say so much about a person's sincerity, confidence, or even manipulation tactics. Manipulators often use eye contact to assert dominance or control conversations. When you understand how to read these cues, you can learn to protect yourself from being deceived by the look someone gives you.

Chapter 6 dived into emotional manipulation—the art of playing with feelings. Guilt, fear, sympathy—these are some of the most potent emotions used by manipulators to get what they want. They know that if they can trigger your emotional responses, they can control your actions. Recognizing these emotional tactics is the first step to staying immune to them. Once you are aware of how guilt-trips or emotional blackmail work, you can break free from the cycle of being manipulated.

Then, we moved to the subtle art of persuasion in Chapter 7. Persuasion isn't inherently evil; in fact, it's a crucial skill. Persuasion can be used ethically, but too often, it's used to manipulate. Learning to differentiate between ethical persuasion and unethical manipulation can help you navigate the world of influence without losing control over your decisions. When persuasion is used ethically, it can lead to more productive conversations and positive outcomes. When used unethically, it leaves you feeling powerless.

In Chapter 8, we learned that silence speaks louder than words. Manipulators will often use silence to create tension, control the conversation, or make you feel pressured. Silence can be one of the most powerful tools in any conversation, whether you're using it to buy time, create space for reflection, or break someone's manipulative grip. The strength of silence comes from the power it gives you to remain calm and collected, unaffected by the emotional noise around you.

Building psychological immunity, as we discussed in Chapter 9, is crucial for protecting yourself from manipulation. Recognizing your psychological triggers and learning to manage your emotions puts you in control. Emotional intelligence isn't just a nice-to-have; it's essential for making intentional decisions that serve your well-being. When you're emotionally resilient, you're less likely to be manipulated by others and more likely to make decisions that align with your true self.

In Chapter 10, we explored the power of choice. When you have multiple options, you reduce the power manipulators have over you. Choice empowers you. It creates a sense of freedom, making you less susceptible to being cornered into making decisions based on someone else's agenda. When you know you have options, the pressure to conform or comply disappears, and you're able to make decisions that truly serve you.

Finally, in Chapter 12, we examined how walking away is the most powerful form of control. Sometimes, the best way to regain control is simply by refusing to engage. Walking away isn't about weakness. It's about knowing when to disengage from toxic situations, preserving your energy, and protecting your peace. By refusing to engage with manipulators, you create space for healthier, more positive interactions.

So, where do we go from here?

The next step is to practice. It's one thing to recognize manipulation, but it's another thing entirely to be able to respond to it in a way that protects your peace. Recognizing manipulation isn't just about identifying tactics in others—it's about recognizing your own triggers and understanding how those triggers influence your reactions. It's about seeing the signs in real-time and knowing how to disengage, step back, and make decisions that align with your best interests.

Start by observing the dynamics of your daily life. This doesn't mean becoming paranoid or constantly looking for hidden motives, but it means being aware. Manipulation is a part of everyday life, whether you're dealing with a family member who uses guilt, a friend who tries to get you to do things you don't want to do, or a colleague who pressures you into agreeing to something.

Next, disengage. It may sound simple, but the strength in walking away from toxic situations or manipulative people is often underestimated. It's easy to get caught up in trying to explain yourself or defend your actions, especially when someone is pushing your emotional buttons. However, the real power lies in choosing to disengage and protect your peace.

When you engage with manipulators, you get pulled into their emotional drama. They know how to push your buttons, trigger your vulnerabilities, and make you feel responsible for their actions or emotions. The more you engage, the more energy you give away. Manipulators thrive on your emotional responses. They want to see you react, feel guilty, or even give in to their demands. By walking away, you're taking away their power. You stop feeding into their agenda, and instead, you take back control over your feelings and decisions.

One of the first things you'll notice when you start disengaging is that your emotions become more manageable. Instead of reacting to every emotional pull or guilt trip, you'll begin to feel more centered and in control. You'll notice that you're able to pause before responding. This pause is crucial. It gives you the space to think and decide how you want to respond rather than simply react. This can feel like a significant shift, but over time, it becomes second nature. You'll find that it's easier to say "no" when something doesn't align with your values or boundaries.

When you stop engaging, you also start to protect your energy. Every time you step into a situation where manipulation is at play, you expend emotional energy. It's like giving away pieces of yourself, and over time, you can start to feel depleted. Disengagement lets you recharge. Instead of getting stuck in a back-and-forth, you create space for your own thoughts, clarity, and peace. The more you practice disengaging, the more you'll realize how vital this space is for your well-being.

Disengagement also creates the mental clarity you need to think more clearly about the situation. When someone is trying to manipulate you, they often introduce confusion. They may twist your words, use emotional pressure, or make you feel uncertain about your decisions. This confusion makes it difficult to assess the situation objectively. When you disengage, you clear away the emotional fog and give yourself the time to see things more clearly. This clarity is a form of empowerment. You can then approach the situation with a fresh perspective and make decisions that are in your best interest.

This sense of clarity also allows you to refocus on what really matters. When manipulators try to distract you with guilt, fear, or shame, it's easy to lose sight of your own goals, values, and needs. Disengagement helps you reconnect with those. By walking away, you remind yourself that your peace, your priorities, and your needs matter. You no longer allow someone else's drama to dictate your actions or decisions.

A major benefit of disengagement is that it teaches you how to set and enforce boundaries. Boundaries are essential for protecting your emotional space. They tell others what you are willing to tolerate and what you are not. When you constantly engage with someone who is trying to manipulate you, your boundaries become blurred. Disengagement is a way to reinforce those boundaries. You don't need to explain yourself or justify your decision to walk away. You simply choose to disengage, and that action alone is enough to assert your boundaries.

Over time, disengaging from manipulators strengthens your ability to set clear boundaries in every area of your life. Whether it's with family, friends, colleagues, or acquaintances, the more you practice disengagement, the more you'll find that your boundaries are respected. People will start to understand that you are someone who values your peace and is unwilling to compromise it for anyone's emotional agenda.

When you disengage, you also reclaim your personal power. Manipulators rely on emotional pressure to control and influence you. By refusing to engage, you demonstrate that you are in control of your emotional state. You don't need to participate in someone else's game of emotional manipulation. Instead, you choose how you respond. This is the heart of empowerment—taking control over your own actions, reactions, and emotions.

Disengaging isn't about running away from difficult situations. It's about choosing not to let those situations dictate your emotional state. It's about knowing when to walk away in order to protect your peace. Walking away is a conscious decision to value your emotional well-being over external pressures. This is a strength that comes from knowing your worth and refusing to let anyone diminish it.

Ultimately, disengagement allows you to create space for healthier interactions. When you stop engaging with someone who manipulates you, you free up emotional and mental space that can be used for more positive and fulfilling connections. Healthy relationships are built on mutual respect and understanding, not emotional manipulation. By practicing disengagement, you create a life that is centered around respect, peace, and empowerment.

As you continue practicing disengagement, you'll notice that your confidence grows. The more you protect your peace and set boundaries, the more you'll trust yourself. You'll no longer feel swayed by manipulative tactics. You'll start to feel empowered in every decision you make, knowing that you have the strength to protect your peace no matter what.

Disengaging is one of the strongest tools you can use to regain control over your life, and it starts with choosing to prioritize your emotional well-being. Once you recognize your ability to disengage, you'll feel more in control of your relationships, your decisions, and your overall peace of mind. It's time to step into this strength, protecting your emotional space and embracing the power of disengagement.

The next step is to continue practicing this power every day, learning from each experience, and growing stronger in your ability to protect your peace. The more you do this, the easier it will become to stay true to your boundaries, values, and emotional needs.

The power of disengagement is yours—now, it's time to use it in every part of your life.

Printed in Dunstable, United Kingdom